Build Location Apps on iOS with Swift

Use Apple Maps, Google Maps, and Mapbox to Code Location Aware Mobile Apps

Jeffrey Linwood

Apress®

Build Location Apps on iOS with Swift: Use Apple Maps, Google Maps, and Mapbox to Code Location Aware Mobile Apps

Jeffrey Linwood
Austin, TX, USA

ISBN-13 (pbk): 978-1-4842-6082-1   ISBN-13 (electronic): 978-1-4842-6083-8
https://doi.org/10.1007/978-1-4842-6083-8

Copyright © 2020 by Jeffrey Linwood

Managing Director, Apress Media LLC: Welmoed Spahr
Acquisitions Editor: Aaron Black
Development Editor: James Markham
Coordinating Editor: Jessica Vakili

Distributed to the book trade worldwide by Springer Science+Business Media New York, 233 Spring Street, 6th Floor, New York, NY 10013. Phone 1-800-SPRINGER, fax (201) 348-4505, e-mail orders-ny@springer-sbm.com, or visit www.springeronline.com. Apress Media, LLC is a California LLC and the sole member (owner) is Springer Science + Business Media Finance Inc (SSBM Finance Inc). SSBM Finance Inc is a **Delaware** corporation.

For information on translations, please e-mail booktranslations@springernature.com; for reprint, paperback, or audio rights, please e-mail bookpermissions@springernature.com.

Apress titles may be purchased in bulk for academic, corporate, or promotional use. eBook versions and licenses are also available for most titles. For more information, reference our Print and eBook Bulk Sales web page at http://www.apress.com/bulk-sales.

Any source code or other supplementary material referenced by the author in this book is available to readers on GitHub via the book's product page, located at www.apress.com/978-1-4842-6082-1. For more detailed information, please visit http://www.apress.com/source-code.

Printed on acid-free paper

Table of Contents

About the Author

Jeffrey Linwood is an experienced software developer who has worked on many iOS and Android apps that use maps or location functionality. He's also taught and mentored college student application teams as they develop their first iOS apps. While teaching, he noticed a lack of good sample applications and tutorials for map and location applications. Jeff also enjoys running, hiking, and spending time with his wife, Clover, in Austin, Texas. You can follow Jeff on Twitter at @jefflinwood, or on his blog, https://www.jefflinwood.com.

About the Technical Reviewer

Felipe Laso is a Senior Systems Engineer working at Lextech Global Services. He's also an aspiring game designer/programmer. You can follow him on Twitter at @iFeliLM or on his blog.

CHAPTER 1

Creating Your First MapKit App

This book will be project based – starting out simple and then getting more complicated. With that in mind, our first iOS app will only be one screen that displays a map. That map will have one pin on it, with the location of my city, Austin, Texas. Feel free to use your own town for this example, of course!

Getting started

The first step is to make sure that you have a recent version of Xcode (at the time of writing, Xcode 11) installed on your Mac. If you're using earlier versions of Xcode, this code may not compile, and you may not be able to follow directions. Xcode is free and may be downloaded from the Mac App Store or from Apple's developer portal.

We'll also be using the Swift programming language, instead of Apple's older programming language for iOS, Objective-C. Almost all of this book would be directly applicable to an Objective-C application. The underlying application programming interfaces (APIs) used in iOS are generally the same.

The Swift language has been evolving since its first release. This book uses Swift 5, which is supported in Xcode 10 and above.

© Jeffrey Linwood 2020
J. Linwood, *Build Location Apps on iOS with Swift*,
https://doi.org/10.1007/978-1-4842-6083-8_1

Go ahead and open up Xcode, and create a new application. We'll be creating a new Single View Application (Figure 1-1).

Figure 1-1. *New project window in Xcode*

Click the Next button, and then name your new project on the options dialog, as seen in Figure 1-2. I'm going to call the new application FirstMapsApp and give it an organization identifier of com. buildingmobileapps.maps and use my name for the Organization Name.

Be sure to choose Swift as the Language.

For this project, we will not be using SwiftUI – we will be using UIKit as the application framework. Leave the SwiftUI check box unchecked.

We do not need to include Core Data in our project – Core Data is an Apple technology used for storing data locally on iOS, and we won't need it for this example. We won't be using Core Data in this book.

You can also uncheck Include Unit Tests and Include UI Tests, as we won't be setting up any tests for this project.

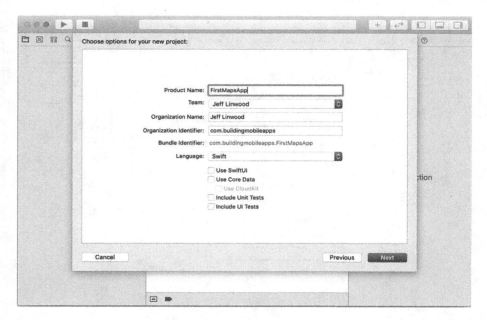

Figure 1-2. *New project options for an iOS app*

Click Next, and save the project in a convenient location. You can create a Git repository for your code if you want, but we won't be directly addressing source control in this book. It's always a good idea to keep up with Git commits as your project goes along, so that you can easily roll back to a working copy.

After saving your project, Xcode will open your project and present an overview of your application (Figure 1-3).

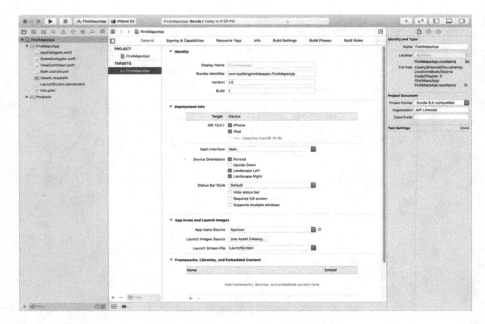

Figure 1-3. *Project overview*

You should now have a working Xcode project – go ahead and run it in one of the iOS Simulators, for instance, the iPhone XR (Figure 1-4).

Figure 1-4. *New iOS application running in a simulator*

You should expect to see a blank screen, as we have not written any code for our application yet. If you do, your development environment is set up and ready to go for the rest of this chapter.

Adding a map

Now it's time to add a map to our view controller. Select the storyboard on the left-hand side; it is the file named `Main.storyboard`. Once the storyboard opens, select the View Controller Scene.

In the upper right-hand corner of your Xcode window, choose the left-most button (the Object library), which is the button with the plus sign in the previous figure, as shown in Figure 1-5.

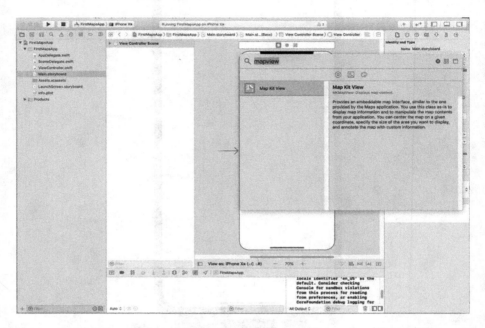

Figure 1-5. *Choosing an MKMapView map from the Object library in Xcode*

Either type Map into the search box underneath the list or scroll down until you find the Map Kit View. Once you have found the Map Kit View, drag it onto your view controller (Figure 1-6).

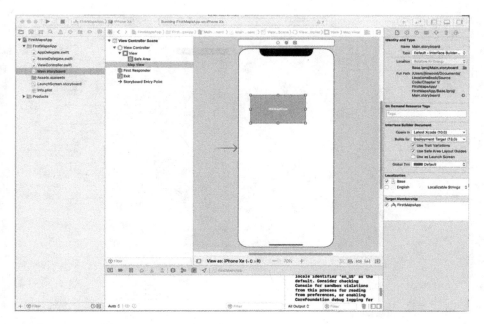

Figure 1-6. *Map View on storyboard*

The map view won't automatically expand to fill the whole screen, so you will need to do that yourself by dragging the edges of the map view to fill the extent of the view. In Figure 1-7, you can see how the map view fills the entire view controller on an iPhone XR device with a notch at the top.

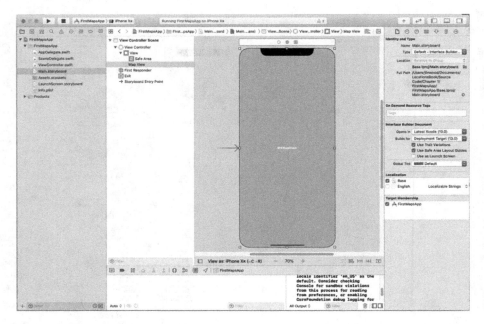

Figure 1-7. *Map View fills view*

Even though we dragged the edges of the map view out to the edges of the view controller's view, that doesn't mean that the map view will use the entire screen on all sizes of the iPhone and iPad. To make the map view fill the view controller's view (also known as its parent view), we will need to add constraints to the map view.

On the right-hand side of the toolbar underneath your view controller, you will see five icons – the first icon is usually grayed out. The third icon (Add New Constraints) opens up the Add New Constraints dialog box, which we can use for our layouts.

Uncheck the "Constrain to margins" check box, as we are going to fill the entire view with the map, not leaving any margins. Go ahead and select the faint dashed red line for all four constraints (top, bottom, left, and right). After selecting them, make sure that all of the values are 0, and press the "Add 4 Constraints" button (Figure 1-8).

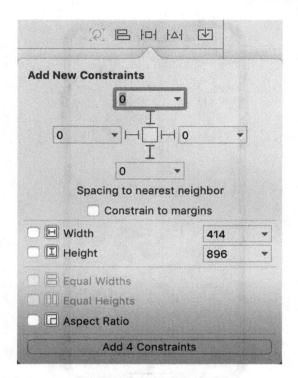

Figure 1-8. *Adding constraints to a Map View*

Your map view will now properly fill up the entire screen on an iPhone or iPad. If you would like to double-check this, select the Map View on the storyboard. Next, choose the fifth icon on the right-hand side, the Size Inspector, and you will see that you have constraints for all four sides of your Map View.

Now try running your iOS app, and you will see that you have a nice, large map on your app – as seen in Figure 1-9.

Figure 1-9. *An iOS app with a full-screen map view*

This was a pretty straightforward process to get the map up and running and didn't even involve writing any code in Swift.

Adding a pin to your map

Now that we have our map, it's time to add a pin that shows our home city!

Before we add the pin to the map, we will need to create an outlet for the map, named `mapView`, using Xcode's Assistant. While you have the `Main.storyboard` editor open, choose the **Assistant** view from the **Editor** menu. You'll see the `ViewController` class open up next to your view controller in the storyboard (Figure 1-10).

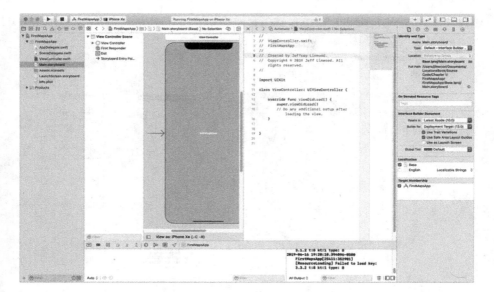

Figure 1-10. *Xcode Editor and Assistant view*

Select the map view on the storyboard or on the outline view, hold
down the Control key, and then drag an outlet into the ViewController
class, as shown in Figure 1-11.

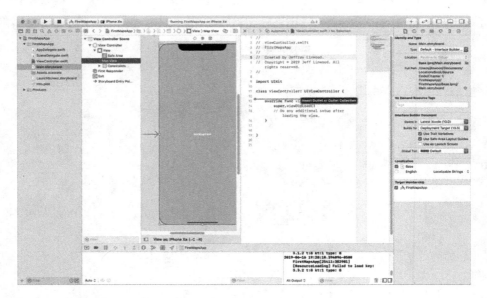

Figure 1-11. *Creating an outlet*

After creating the outlet, name the outlet `mapView` in the dialog box that appears (Figure 1-12).

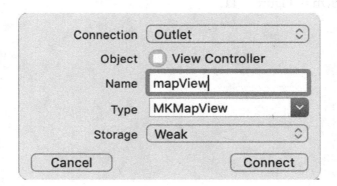

Figure 1-12. *Naming the outlet*

You'll notice that the `ViewController` class will no longer compile – that is because our map is an `MKMapView`, part of the `MapKit` framework. We need to import this framework into our `ViewController` class so that we can use classes from the MapKit framework. Otherwise, Xcode will show errors when we try and build our project.

Add the following line right below the import UIKit statement to import the MapKit framework.

```
import MapKit
```

Beyond maps themselves, the MapKit framework has a wide range of functionality. With MapKit, we represent locations on the map as annotations. Annotations implement the MKAnnotation protocol, which consists of a latitude and longitude coordinate pair and an optional title and subtitle. The MapKit framework comes with a basic implementation of MKAnnotation, the MKPointAnnotation class, but for most apps, you will want to create your own implementation of MKAnnotation. In this chapter, we will use MKPointAnnotation, but the later chapters of this book will use our own implementation, so you can see how it works both ways.

Once you have an annotation (or many annotations), you can just add it to the map using the addAnnotation() or addAnnotations() method on the MKMapView class.

Annotations are not the actual pin that the map displays – those are annotation views, which are subclasses of the MKAnnotationView class. By default, you will get an MKPinAnnotationView, which is the standard red pin that you see in many mapping apps. You can customize the pin color a little, but for most apps, you will want to put in your custom images. We'll use our own custom images in the next chapters of this book.

To create an annotation as an MKPointAnnotation, we do need to be able to create a coordinate, which we can do with CLLocationCoordinate2DMake(). For our purposes in this chapter, we are going to add all of the code to the viewDidLoad() method in the ViewController class. Xcode created this method for you when you generated a new project.

This method is currently empty except for a call to super.viewDidLoad(). Leave that line of code in the viewDidLoad() method, and place this code beneath that.

Pass in the latitude and the longitude (as double values) to create the coordinate. The `MKPointAnnotation` will need this coordinate set, such as in the following code:

```
let austin = MKPointAnnotation()
austin.coordinate = CLLocationCoordinate2DMake(30.25, -97.75)
```

The longitude for Austin is going to be negative, because Austin, Texas, is in the Western Hemisphere. The latitude is positive because the city is in the Northern Hemisphere.

To give the annotation a title, we can simply set the title property

```
austin.title = "Austin"
```

And then after setting the title and coordinate properties, we can call one method on the map view to add the annotation

```
mapView.addAnnotation(austin)
```

Run this class (Listing 1-1), and you will see the iPhone app displaying the Austin pin, after you scroll the map to show Texas on your Simulator. Go ahead and change the pin to your city or to any other location you want. Add more pins for different locations!

Listing 1-1. The ViewController class with a pin that displays on the Map view

```
import UIKit
import MapKit

class ViewController: UIViewController {

    @IBOutlet weak var mapView: MKMapView!
    override func viewDidLoad() {
        super.viewDidLoad()
        // Do any additional setup after loading the view.
```

```
    let austin = MKPointAnnotation()
    austin.coordinate = CLLocationCoordinate2DMake(30.25,
    -97.75)
    austin.title = "Austin"
    mapView.addAnnotation(austin)
  }
}
```

Figure 1-13 shows the iPhone app with the Austin pin.

Figure 1-13. *The completed iOS app, showing the pin for Austin on the map*

Summary

We have now created an iOS application that shows a pin on a map. Along the way, we have covered the `MapKit` framework, map views, and annotations.

In the next chapter, we will build on the basic map application we built here and display the user's location on the map. If you would like to try a similar project to this example out with the Google Maps for iOS SDK or the Mapbox SDK, please see Chapters 7 and 11, respectively.

CHAPTER 2

Getting the User's Location

Let's take our app one step further and show the user's location on the map. The location functionality in iOS is extremely powerful – you can get the user's current location, or you can track the user's location as it changes over time to show their path on a map. We will use the CoreLocation framework for this, as well as the MapKit framework we discussed earlier.

We will add additional functionality to the project from Chapter 1. That FirstMapsApp project already has the map view in place that we will use to show the user's location.

Privacy and location permissions

Because an app can do so much with the user's location, Apple has added protections for the user's privacy that you as an application developer need to understand.

An iOS app can request permission to use the user's location while the application is in use or while the application is in the background. You may have seen these alerts pop up when you use location-based apps on an iPhone or iPad yourself. If your app doesn't have a compelling reason to get the user's location, the user is very likely to not allow the app access.

© Jeffrey Linwood 2020
J. Linwood, *Build Location Apps on iOS with Swift*,
https://doi.org/10.1007/978-1-4842-6083-8_2

If your app relies on using the user's location in the background, iOS will pop up a confirmation alert to the user that says your app is continuing to use their location in the background, and would they like to continue providing their location? Many users will turn off location sharing at that point.

Location permissions in the Info.plist file

Your iOS app will require modifications in two places to access the user's location – the Info.plist application configuration file and your app delegate or a view controller. The Info.plist will need to have values for one or both of two keys, depending on which location access your app needs – when in use or always:

- NSLocationWhenInUseUsageDescription
- NSLocationAlwaysAndWhenInUseUsageDescription

These settings are configurable through the Xcode Property List Editor, so you do not have to edit the plist directly in XML. You also don't need to know these exact key definitions – in the Property List Editor, the descriptions are listed as Privacy - Location When In Use Usage Description and Privacy - Location Always and When In Use Usage Description.

Select the Info.plist file in Xcode. The Property List Editor appears, as in Figure 2-1.

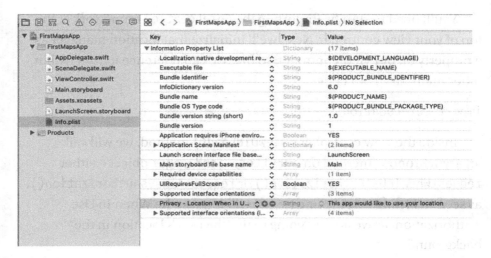

Figure 2-1. *Location privacy in Info.plist*

Any text can be used as the value of these keys – it will be displayed to the user after your app asks for location permission from the user. Go ahead and add a row to the Info.plist file and then set the key to be `Privacy - Location When In Use Description` and the value to "This app would like to use your location". That leads us to the next step in this chapter – requesting permission from the user.

Requesting location permissions from the end user

Now that you have decided whether to ask for permission to track the user's location when the application is in use, or at all times, and you have configured the `Info.plist` file with your corresponding definition, the next step is to ask the user for permission programmatically. This requires creating a `CLLocationManager` object and then requesting the appropriate permission from the user.

You'll need to start by importing the CoreLocation framework at the top of your view controller. Next, we'll initialize that location manager as a property on our view controller, so that we can reference it from within other methods in our code.

```
import CoreLocation
```

Inside the view controller's viewDidLoad() method, we will call an asynchronous method on our CLLocationManager object – either requestWhenInUseAuthorization() or requestAlwaysAuthorization(), as seen in Listing 2-1. In our case, we will request the When In Use Authorization, as we are not going to use the user's location in the background.

Listing 2-1. Requesting location authorization with CoreLocation

```
import UIKit
import MapKit
import CoreLocation

class ViewController: UIViewController {

  @IBOutlet weak var mapView: MKMapView!

  var locationManager:CLLocationManager!

  override func viewDidLoad() {
    super.viewDidLoad()
    // Do any additional setup after loading the view.
    let austin = MKPointAnnotation()
    austin.coordinate = CLLocationCoordinate2DMake(30.25, -97.75)
    austin.title = "Austin"
    mapView.addAnnotation(austin)
```

```
    locationManager = CLLocationManager.init()
    locationManager.requestWhenInUseAuthorization()
  }
}
```

After adding these lines to the view controller, when you run the application, you should see something similar to the dialog in Figure 2-2 appear.

Figure 2-2. *Location permission dialog in iOS*

To see this dialog again after choosing to allow or deny permission, you will need to delete the compiled app from your phone or iOS Simulator.

Requesting location updates

The next step for your application should be to begin getting location updates if the user has authorized you to do so. To do that, you will need to implement a method from the CLLocationManagerDelegate protocol – lo cationManager(_:didChangeAuthorization:) – which we will do in an extension.

Extensions are a way of organizing the methods in our class around the protocols that we need to implement. This helps avoid some of the code organization problems that come with putting all of your code for a screen into a view controller class. In this particular case, we can make an extension for the CLLocationManagerDelegate protocol and implement the locationManager(_:didChangeAuthorization:) method:

```
extension ViewController: CLLocationManagerDelegate {
  func locationManager(_
    manager: CLLocationManager,
    didChangeAuthorization status: CLAuthorizationStatus) {

  }
}
```

Just implementing this method won't do anything – you will need to tell your location manager that it has a delegate as well, before requesting authorization in the viewDidLoad() method:

```
locationManager = CLLocationManager.init()
locationManager.delegate = self
locationManager.requestWhenInUseAuthorization()
```

Last, it would be nice to see what the user's status is – so we will implement a switch method for each of the different location authorization statuses. The code for the ViewController class is in Listing 2-2.

Listing 2-2. Displaying the location authorization status from within the app

```
import UIKit
import MapKit
import CoreLocation

class ViewController: UIViewController {

  @IBOutlet weak var mapView: MKMapView!

  var locationManager:CLLocationManager!

  override func viewDidLoad() {
    super.viewDidLoad()
    // Do any additional setup after loading the view.
    let austin = MKPointAnnotation()
    austin.coordinate = CLLocationCoordinate2DMake(30.25, -97.75)
    austin.title = "Austin"
    mapView.addAnnotation(austin)

    locationManager = CLLocationManager.init()
    locationManager.delegate = self
    locationManager.requestWhenInUseAuthorization()
  }
}

extension ViewController: CLLocationManagerDelegate {
  func locationManager(_
    manager: CLLocationManager,
    didChangeAuthorization status: CLAuthorizationStatus) {
    switch status {
      case .authorizedWhenInUse:
        print("Authorized When in Use")
```

```
    case .authorizedAlways:
      print("Authorized Always")
    case .denied:
      print("Denied")
    case .notDetermined:
      print("Not determined")
    case .restricted:
      print("Restricted")
    @unknown default:
      print("Unknown status")
  }
 }
}
```

After compiling and running this class, you should see debug output from the location authorization status. It will say "Not Determined" at first, and then after choosing to allow or deny permission to get your location, you will see the corresponding status.

All of that is basic boilerplate code for using the user's location. Let's make it a little more real by showing the user's location on the map!

Displaying the user's location on the map

Open up Main.storyboard, and select the map in the outline view if it is not already selected. We will need to set one property on the map view through Xcode.

Choose the fifth tab (the Attribute Inspector), as seen in Figure 2-3. At the top, one of the check boxes will be for User Location – check that box.

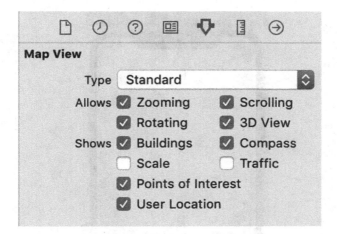

Figure 2-3. *User Location check box on Map View*

That's it! If you are running this on your Simulator, make sure you are sending a location to the app – that setting is on the Simulator's menu, under Features, and then Location. Choose Apple if you want to have an easy setting, or set the coordinates manually.

Go ahead and run the application – it should look similar to Figure 2-4, and the blue dot will be animating.

Figure 2-4. *User Location on map*

That's really all you have to do to get a nice animated user location on to your map. Even though it is only one check box on the map view, you still need to implement all of the CoreLocation framework privacy and permissions code in your view controller.

Summary

We've discussed user privacy for locations and how to use the CoreLocation framework to request authorization from the app's end user. You've also seen how easy it is to show user locations on MapKit maps in iOS.

In our next chapter, we are going to display points of interest on a MapKit app and customize the display for each of those using annotations.

CHAPTER 3

Displaying Annotations on a MapKit Map

In Chapter 1, your first iOS map application displayed one point on the map, with the default red pin at its location. The MapKit framework is capable of much more when it comes to displaying annotations. We can customize the images for the annotations and the callouts seen when a user taps on an annotation.

Let's continue building on top of the FirstMapsApp project that we created in Chapter 1 and then added user locations in Chapter 2.

Understanding MapKit and annotations

The MapKit framework maintains a distinction between annotations – the data displayed on the map – and annotation views, the user interface elements that appear on top of the map at a given coordinate for an annotation. While MapKit provides the MKPointAnnotation class for basic point display, most map applications will use a custom implementation of the MKAnnotation protocol.

© Jeffrey Linwood 2020
J. Linwood, *Build Location Apps on iOS with Swift*,
https://doi.org/10.1007/978-1-4842-6083-8_3

Similarly, `MapKit` also includes the `MKPinAnnotationView` and `MKMarkerAnnotationView` classes for displaying pins or markers on the app. The `MKAnnotationView` class is useful for displaying your own custom images. You can subclass the `MKAnnotationView` class or use it directly.

The `mapView(_:viewFor:)` function on the `MKMapViewDelegate` protocol allows your application to map `MKAnnotationView` objects to `MKAnnotation` objects. Because the `MKPointAnnotation` class has a limited number of data fields, using your own implementation of `MKAnnotation` gives you the most flexibility.

Using a custom annotation class

Implementing your own annotation class is straightforward – you will need to extend the `NSObject` class and then implement the `MKAnnotation` protocol.

The `title` and `subtitle` properties of the `MKAnnotation` protocol are `String` optionals. The `coordinate` property is a little more complicated, as `MapKit` requires that it supports key-value observing (KVO). In practice, this means that it is not a simple declaration with a `var` keyword, but instead you would also have to state that it uses dynamic dispatch with the Objective-C runtime. Your declaration in code would look like this:

```
@objc dynamic var coordinate: CLLocationCoordinate2D
```

A basic custom annotation class, with an `init` method, would look like Listing 3-1.

Listing 3-1. An implementation of an annotation class in Swift

```
import UIKit
import MapKit

class MapPoint: NSObject, MKAnnotation {
  @objc dynamic var coordinate: CLLocationCoordinate2D
  var title:String?
  var subtitle: String?

  init(coordinate:CLLocationCoordinate2D,
       title:String?, subtitle:String?) {
    self.coordinate = coordinate
    self.title = title
    self.subtitle = subtitle
  }
}
```

We will be using this MapPoint class and then later extending it through the course of this chapter. It's likely that you would add additional fields to this annotation class for your specific application. Go ahead and create a new file in your Xcode project named MapPoint.swift, and add the code in Listing 3-1.

Display custom annotations

As the MapPoint class implements the MKAnnotation protocol, your code simply needs to construct new MapPoint objects and then add them to the map view as annotations.

We will create two points on the map, with generic titles and subtitles. Add the code in Listing 3-2 to the end of your viewDidLoad() method in the ViewController class.

Listing 3-2. Displaying custom annotations on a map view

```
let point1 = MapPoint(
  coordinate: CLLocationCoordinate2D(latitude: 33.0,
    longitude: -97.0),
  title: "Point 1",
  subtitle: "Description 1"
)
mapView.addAnnotation(point1)

let point2 = MapPoint(
  coordinate: CLLocationCoordinate2D(latitude: 32.0,
    longitude: -98.0),
  title: "Point 2",
  subtitle: "Description 2"
)
mapView.addAnnotation(point2)
```

After adding this code and running your project, you will not see anything too different from our earlier chapters. We have not customized the view for the annotations yet.

Customizing pins for annotations

The easiest way to change the view displayed for each annotation is to use the MKPinAnnotationView class. Your code can set the pin color in the mapView(_:viewFor:) function. This function comes from the MKMapViewDelegate, so you will need to set the delegate on the map view to either a custom class or to the current view controller. For the purposes of this chapter, we will create an extension to our view controller class that implements the MKMapViewDelegate and then set the delegate on the map view in code, in the viewDidLoad() method.

Add the following line of code to your `viewDidLoad()` method for the map view delegate (you can also set it in the storyboard, if you want):

```
mapView.delegate = self
```

Next, add an extension that implements the map view delegate to the bottom of your view controller class. We will add the `mapView(_:viewFor:)` function to this extension:

```
extension ViewController:MKMapViewDelegate {

}
```

The `mapView(_:viewFor:)` function returns an `MKAnnotationView` for a given `MKAnnotation` instance. We will create a pin annotation view and then do a little customization by setting the pin color to blue, as shown in Listing 3-3.

Listing 3-3. Using a pin annotation view

```
extension ViewController:MKMapViewDelegate {
  func mapView(_ mapView: MKMapView,
      viewFor annotation: MKAnnotation) ->
      MKAnnotationView? {
    let pin = MKPinAnnotationView(
      annotation: annotation,
      reuseIdentifier: "Pin")
    pin.pinTintColor = UIColor.blue
    return pin
  }
}
```

After including this code, you should see blue pins appear on the map in the state of Texas in the United States, as in Figure 3-1. If you worked through Chapter 2 and used that as a base, you will also see a blue pin over your user location. Feel free to adjust the points added to the map for your own location, of course!

Figure 3-1. *Changing the annotations to display as blue pins*

Now that we've demonstrated basic view annotation features, let's move on to some more advanced functionality. The first thing to change will be that the user's location is now showing up as a pin.

Handling the user location

We generally want to keep the user location displaying as a pulsating blue dot, as appears by default. In our code, we can check to see if the annotation we provide a view for is an MKUserLocation annotation – the current location of the user:

```
if annotation is MKUserLocation {
    return nil
}
```

This check would typically be done at the beginning of the mapView(_:viewFor:) function. When you return nil, the map will display the default annotation view.

Add the MKUserLocation check to the beginning of the mapView(_:viewFor:) method and then run the project again – the user location (if you have location enabled) will be the glowing blue dot, not a pin.

Reusing annotation views

While this code works, it could be improved. Similar to table views and reusable table view cells, map views support reusable annotations.

When working with annotation views, it's important to use a reuse identifier. This allows the map view to recycle view objects as the user scrolls through the map. Some annotations will fall out of the visible rectangle of the map, and those views can be recycled for annotations that are now visible. Reusing these annotation views will allow for smooth scrolling, especially with large sets of annotations.

The MKMapView class has a dequeueReusableAnnotationView() function that takes a reuse identifier as an argument. If an annotation view is waiting in the reuse queue, you will get that instance. Any customizations you need to make to that annotation view (for instance, setting the annotation to the current annotation) should be done inside an if let block that checks if an instance was available.

If an instance wasn't available in the reuse queue, you will need to create an annotation view and then properly configure it.

We can improve our annotation view code from Listing 3-3 by reusing views if they are available. Replace the method you already created in the map view delegate extension with the code in Listing 3-4. We also include the check for the MKUserLocation annotation.

Listing 3-4. Reusing annotation views

```
func mapView(_ mapView: MKMapView, viewFor annotation:
MKAnnotation)
  -> MKAnnotationView? {
  if annotation is MKUserLocation {
    return nil
  }

  let reuseId = "Pin"
  var pin: MKPinAnnotationView
  if let reusedPin =
      mapView.dequeueReusableAnnotationView(
      withIdentifier: reuseId)
    as? MKPinAnnotationView {
    pin = reusedPin
    pin.annotation = annotation
  } else {
    pin = MKPinAnnotationView(annotation: annotation,
      reuseIdentifier: reuseId)
    pin.pinTintColor = UIColor.blue
  }
  return pin
}
```

While this code is more complicated than the previous code listing, scrolling the map will be much smoother if you have many annotations displayed on the map.

Dequeuing and creating annotation views

We can simplify the code in Listing 3-4 by letting the map view either dequeue a reusable annotation view or create a new annotation view for us automatically. Your code will need to register the annotation view class with the map view for the reuse identifier, using the `registerClass :forAnnotationViewWithReuseIdentifier:` function on the `MKMapView` class. Our code would use the following line of code in the `viewDidLoad()` method:

```
mapView.register(MKPinAnnotationView.self,
forAnnotationViewWithReuseIdentifier: "Pin")
```

After registering the pin annotation view class with the map view, we can remove the pin annotation view creation code from the `viewFor()` method that we implemented in the `MKMapViewDelegate` extension. This leads to the simpler implementation shown in Listing 3-5.

Listing 3-5. Simplified annotation reuse and creation after registering annotation view with map view

```
override func viewDidLoad() {
  ...
  mapView.register(MKPinAnnotationView.self,
    forAnnotationViewWithReuseIdentifier: "Pin")
}
```

```
func mapView(_ mapView: MKMapView,
  viewFor annotation: MKAnnotation) -> MKAnnotationView? {
  if annotation is MKUserLocation {
    return nil
  }

  let reuseId = "Pin"

  if let pin = mapView.dequeueReusableAnnotationView(
      withIdentifier: reuseId)
    as? MKPinAnnotationView {

    pin.annotation = annotation
    pin.pinTintColor = UIColor.blue
    return pin
  } else {
    return nil
  }
}
```

This has cleaned up our code considerably and would allow us to easily add additional annotation view types if we had multiple types of markers on our map.

Setting images on annotation views

Some of your map application ideas may work fine with the built-in pin or marker annotation view classes. However, it's likely that you will need to use the MKAnnotationView class so that you can set your own images.

We will change our code slightly to create annotation views for a dog park. The reuse identifier will be "DogPark", and we will also have an image of a dog in a park, stored in our iOS app's assets. This image will also be named "DogPark". You will need to download your own image and place it into your Xcode project's assets, so that you have something to display.

In the viewDidLoad() function, add this code:

```
mapView.register(MKAnnotationView.self,
forAnnotationViewWithReuseIdentifier: "DogPark")
```

Next, change the contents of the viewFor() function. This code is simplified, as we don't need to downcast the dequeued annotation view any more. We can also simply return the optional value from this function. The only other change we make is to set the UIImage on the annotation view, instead of changing the pin tint color. The complete changes are shown in Listing 3-6.

Listing 3-6. Use an image on the annotation view

```
func mapView(_ mapView: MKMapView,
  viewFor annotation: MKAnnotation)
    -> MKAnnotationView? {
  if annotation is MKUserLocation {
    return nil
  }

  let reuseId = "DogPark"
  let view = mapView.dequeueReusableAnnotationView(
      withIdentifier: reuseId)
  view?.annotation = annotation
  view?.image = UIImage(named:"DogPark")
  return view
}
```

After you replace the code that dequeued the reusable pin annotation views with Listing 3-6, run the project. You will see the dog park image appear in place of your pins.

Using callouts with annotations

After using a custom image for your annotation, it's likely that you will want to display a callout when a user taps on your annotation. The canShowCallout property of the MKAnnotationView controls whether or not this is shown. When creating the view for the annotation, add the following line of code:

```
view?.canShowCallout = true
```

And then run your application. After tapping on an annotation, you will see a pop-up with the title and subtitle that you set, as shown in Figure 3-2.

Figure 3-2. *Using images and callouts for the annotations*

As you can see, the way you display annotations on your map is extremely customizable. Try changing up the images for each annotation based on a data point, or try displaying some as images and some as pins.

Summary

In this chapter, we've built on the mapping fundamentals from Chapter 1 to customize the markers we display on the map. We've seen how to use reusable annotation views to improve performance for maps with many markers.

In the next chapter, we will discuss how to use Apple's local search functionality to provide points of interest from their database for your map.

CHAPTER 4

Searching for Points of Interest

Apple has its own database of places and addresses that you can use with your iOS application. Your code can call an instance of the MKLocalSearch class to get points of interest that you can then display on a map view. This makes it easy to implement search functionality based on what geographic region is currently displaying in the map.

Create a new Swift iOS project in Xcode with the Single View Application template. Name your application SearchingForPointsOfInterest. Go ahead and add a map view to the only screen in the storyboard, and connect it to an outlet called mapView on the ViewController class. Also import the MapKit framework, if you haven't done so. These are the steps we've followed in the previous chapters, so they should be pretty straightforward.

Getting started with local search

Apple's local search functionality for MapKit isn't a web-accessible API that you can call with an HTTP request, unlike other integrations you may be using in your application. Apple provides two helper classes – MKLocalSearch and MKLocalSearch.Request – for working with local search. Use an MKLocalSearch.Request instance to define what to search for, and then use MKLocalSearch to execute the request and return the results.

© Jeffrey Linwood 2020
J. Linwood, *Build Location Apps on iOS with Swift*,
https://doi.org/10.1007/978-1-4842-6083-8_4

The first step is to construct the search request:

```
let searchRequest = MKLocalSearch.Request()
```

The search request object has four different properties you may use to filter down the results:

- `naturalLanguageQuery` – This is a word or phrase that the service will use to find results, such as "park" or "art museum".

- `region` – This is a map region, typically the region of a map on the current screen – useful for limiting search results to a geographic location.

- `pointOfInterestFilter` – Only display points of interest that match one or more of the different types in the `MKPointOfInterestCategory` struct. For instance, beaches, restaurants, and stores are all different categories.

- `resultTypes` – Local search can return addresses, points of interest, or both.

Not all of these need to be set to use local search – typically your map application would use `naturalLanguageQuery` and `region`. If you do not set the region, the local search will use the device's location for the search. You do not need to ask for location permissions to use local search.

If we set the natural language query on the search request, the code will look like this:

```
searchRequest.naturalLanguageQuery = "coffee"
```

The search request object describes the search we want to do – the `MKLocalSearch` object will run the search. There are two steps to running a search – creating the `MKLocalSearch` instance with a search request object and then calling the `start` method on the local search. Listing 4-1 contains an example of each of these steps.

With the `MKLocalSearch.Request` object we created earlier, the initialization of an `MKLocalSearch` instance looks like this:

```
let search = MKLocalSearch(request: searchRequest)
```

The `start` method takes a completion handler as the only argument. The completion handler will run on the main thread in your iOS app and has two optional arguments – a response of type `MKLocalSearch.Response` and an error of type `Error`.

The response will consist of an array of `MKMapItem` map items with the results of the search and a map region that includes all of the results. You could set the map view on the screen to the new region if you wanted to display all results, or you could let the user scroll themselves to find results if you had an alternative search results display (such as a list).

Listing 4-1. Searching for points of interest with MKLocalSearch

```
let searchRequest = MKLocalSearch.Request()
searchRequest.naturalLanguageQuery = "coffee"

let search = MKLocalSearch(request: searchRequest)
search.start { (response, error) in
  guard let response = response else {
    print("Error searching - no response")
    if let error = error {
      print("Error: \(error.localizedDescription)")
    } else {
      print("No error specified")
    }
    return
  }
```

```
  for mapItem in response.mapItems {
    print(mapItem.name ?? "No name specified")
  }
}
```

Checking that the response is provided in the callback using guard let allows you to display an error to the user. For this code, the results will be found in the debug console, but you could display an alert message to the user.

Exploring the map items in the response

The local search results will consist of MKMapItem objects. Each of these map items in the result is a point of interest and contains location and address information in a placemark object, a point of interest category, and if available, the name, phone number, URL, and time zone for the map item. These MKMapItem objects are also used for directions and routing, as we will see in Chapter 5.

The placemark objects are from the MKPlacemark class and contain latitude, longitude, and street address information. These placemarks implement the MKAnnotation protocol discussed in Chapter 3. This means that you can add placemarks directly to a map view to display results.

Displaying the search results on a map

Now that you have learned the relationship between map items and annotations, it's easy to see how these search results can be displayed on the map view. Be sure you have a map view on your storyboard and an outlet variable named mapView on your ViewController class before trying this code.

The previous code listing has been enhanced to work with the map view – the changes are in bold in the following code listing.

Listing 4-2. Displaying search results on the map

```
let searchRequest = MKLocalSearch.Request()
searchRequest.naturalLanguageQuery = "coffee"
searchRequest.region = mapView.region

let search = MKLocalSearch(request: searchRequest)
search.start { (response, error) in
  guard let response = response else {
    print("Error searching - no response")
    if let error = error {
      print("Error: \(error.localizedDescription)")
    } else {
      print("No error specified")
    }
    return
  }

  for mapItem in response.mapItems {
    self.mapView.addAnnotation(mapItem.placemark)
  }
self.mapView.setRegion(response.boundingRegion, animated: true)
 }
```

The changes in the preceding code listing accomplish a few things. The first change sets the region used in the search request to be the current region displaying in the map view. The second change adds the map item's placemark as an annotation, instead of printing the name to the debug console. The last change sets the boundaries of the visible region on the map view to the region that contains all search results.

Create a new function named showCoffeeOnMap() and put the code in Listing 4-2 into this function. Then call your new function from the viewDidLoad() function in your ViewController class. Go ahead and run this application in the Simulator or on your device. You should see results similar to the following screenshot, depending on how much coffee is for sale in your area.

Figure 4-1. *Displaying search results on a map view*

Creating annotations for results

One downside of adding the placemark directly as an annotation is that Apple uses the street address of the placemark as the title for the annotation, instead of using the name from the map item. This is not the best user experience, so let's modify our code a little bit to create a new annotation from each map item, as seen in Listing 4-3.

Listing 4-3. Create an annotation for each search result

```
for mapItem in response.mapItems {
  let annotation = MKPointAnnotation()
  annotation.coordinate =
    mapItem.placemark.coordinate

  annotation.title = mapItem.name
  annotation.subtitle = mapItem.phoneNumber

  self.mapView.addAnnotation(annotation)
}
```

Replace the existing for loop with the preceding code block, and you will see the names of the coffee shops, rather than just the street addresses.

Filtering with points of interest categories

Apple's search works well with the natural language query, whether you look for something generic or something more specific. However, if your application will be looking for points of interest in categories that Apple has defined, then using the point of interest filter will improve your user's experience.

Set the point of interest filter on the search request with an instance of the `MKPointOfInterestFilter` class. This filter is new to iOS 13 and isn't available in previous versions of iOS. When you create a point of interest filter, you have two choices – you can create a filter that includes only one or more categories, or you can create a filter that excludes one or more categories. Typically, you would probably be using the inclusion filter, but if your search results are being populated with irrelevant results from categories that don't fit your app, it's certainly easy to exclude categories.

The `MKPointOfInterestCategory` struct defines all of the different categories you can use. A partial list follows:

- Airport

- Amusement Park

- Aquarium

- ATM

- Bakery

- Bank

- Beach

- Brewery

And so forth, down to the zoo category. As you can see, if you are building an application that relies on local search, these filters could be quite useful.

To use an `MKPointOfInterestFilter` class with the `MKLocalSearch.Request` search request, you just need to set the `pointOfInterestFilter` property. For instance, to perform a search for local bakeries, use the following code:

```
searchRequest.pointOfInterestFilter =
  MKPointOfInterestFilter(including: [.bakery])
```

If we were to combine this point of interest filter with the preceding code listing that creates annotations from the local search map item results and then remove the natural language query string, we would have a function that looks like Listing 4-4.

Listing 4-4. Category filter with map annotations

```
let searchRequest = MKLocalSearch.Request()
searchRequest.pointOfInterestFilter =
  MKPointOfInterestFilter(including: [.bakery])
searchRequest.region = mapView.region

let search = MKLocalSearch(request: searchRequest)
search.start { (response, error) in
  guard let response = response else {
    print("Error searching - no response")
    if let error = error {
      print("Error: \(error.localizedDescription)")
    } else {
      print("No error specified")
    }
    return
  }

  for mapItem in response.mapItems {
    let annotation = MKPointAnnotation()
    annotation.coordinate =
      mapItem.placemark.coordinate
```

```
    annotation.title = mapItem.name
    annotation.subtitle = mapItem.phoneNumber
    self.mapView.addAnnotation(annotation)
  }

  self.mapView.setRegion(response.boundingRegion, animated: true)
}
```

Running this code on your iOS app will yield similar results to this screenshot, depending on how many bakeries are in your area.

Figure 4-2. *Points of interest from a category filter with annotations*

Working with local search is fairly straightforward, as the
`MKLocalSearch` class that Apple provides does not have any advanced
functionality, such as pagination of search results. Creating your own
annotations from map items in the search results generally makes the
most sense. Using the techniques in Chapter 3, you can create custom
annotation views, for instance, to match the categories for the points of
interest.

In the next chapter, we will use Apple's directions API to create routes
for driving or walking. The directions API also uses the `MKMapItem` class,
and we will explore other functionality for map items that wasn't covered
in this chapter, such as user location and opening map items in the Apple
Maps app.

CHAPTER 5

Getting Directions with MapKit

Providing walking or driving directions from one place to another inside your application is easy with MapKit. You can also instruct the Apple Maps app to open up and route the user to a location – this could be useful if you think the user might just prefer to use a dedicated app.

Create another Swift iOS project in Xcode with the Single View Application template. Name your application `DirectionsMapKitApp`. Go ahead and add a map view to the only screen in the storyboard, and connect it to an outlet called `mapView` on the `ViewController` class. In the view controller, import the `MapKit` framework, along with `UIKit`.

You can also reuse one of the projects from an earlier chapter if you like, as those will be set up with the map view.

Understanding the Directions API

Similar to local search, the directions API isn't a publicly available REST API. Instead, the Apple directions functionality is accessed through `MapKit` classes. If you happen to have a web version of your application, Apple also provides directions through `MapKit` for JavaScript, but that product is outside the scope of this book.

© Jeffrey Linwood 2020
J. Linwood, *Build Location Apps on iOS with Swift*,
https://doi.org/10.1007/978-1-4842-6083-8_5

To use the directions API, you will use an instance of the `MKDirections` class. Initialize that instance with an `MKDirections.Request` object that specifies which directions you want to request, and then make an asynchronous call to the Apple servers with either the `calculate()` or `calculateETA()` method. The `calculate()` method takes a completion handler to use as a callback with either an `MKDirections.Response` object or an `Error` object.

The response will contain one or more routes to follow. Typically, you might just want to request one route, but you can request alternate routes in your directions request – doing this will give you multiple routes if there are any.

These routes are `MKRoute` objects, and they contain several things that would be useful for displaying routes to a user – the route geometry, which can be added to the map view as an overlay, a list of route steps (as `MKRouteStep` objects), the total distance, and the expected travel time.

Let's illustrate how these classes work together with a simple example for driving directions.

Getting started with directions

We'll need to start by creating a directions request object. Create a new method named `getDirections()` in your view controller class, and then place a call to that method in your `viewDidLoad()` method. Add the following line of code to the `getDirections()` method to create a directions request object:

```
let request = MKDirections.Request()
```

All of the code from this section of the chapter is listed out in full in Listing 5-1.

MKDirections.Request can take a source and a destination – both of which need to be MKMapItem objects. We discussed the MKMapItem class in Chapter 4. You can certainly use an MKMapItem instance that comes from a local search, or you can create your own MKMapItem objects from an MKPlacemark instance. Placemarks can be created from Core Location coordinates.

We'll need to do this for both the source and the destination. Because there is some repeatable code, we can abstract this out to a helper function:

```
func createMapItem(latitude:Double,
   longitude:Double) -> MKMapItem {
   let coord = CLLocationCoordinate2D(
     latitude: latitude,
     longitude: longitude)
   let placemark = MKPlacemark(coordinate: coord)
   return MKMapItem(placemark: placemark)
}
```

Once we have this helper function, creating map items for the source and destination properties looks like the following code, which you can add to the getDirections() method:

```
request.source = createMapItem(latitude: 40.7128, longitude: -74)
request.destination = createMapItem(latitude: 38.91, longitude:
-77.037)
```

These coordinates happen to be for New York City (as the source) and Washington, DC (as the destination). Feel free to replace these with your own start and end points, as long as it's feasible to drive between them.

The directions request takes a transportation type for the request. These direction types are enumerated in the `MKDirectionsTransportType` struct and include

- `MKDirectionsTransportType.automobile`

- `MKDirectionsTransportType.walking`

- `MKDirectionsTransportType.transit`

- `MKDirectionsTransportType.any`

Typically, you would specify one of automobile, walking, or transit, similar to the Apple Maps iOS app. In your `getDirections()` function, add the following line of code:

```
request.transportType = .automobile
```

After setting up the directions request with a source, direction, and transport type, you can create an `MKDirections` object from the directions request:

```
let directions = MKDirections(request: request)
```

Next, you can call the `calculate()` or the `calculateETA()` method on the `MKDirections` object. Both are asynchronous and take a completion handler as the only argument. In our case, we are interested in getting the complete results, including steps, a graphic for the route, and the time and distance, so we will use the `calculate()` method. The following code sets us up by unwrapping the response:

```
directions.calculate { (response, error) in
  guard let response = response else {
    print(error ?? "No error found")
    return
  }
}
```

We'll pass a closure to the `calculate()` method. The closure takes two arguments – an optional `MKDirections.Response` and an optional `Error`. We'll check to make sure that the response exists with a `guard let` statement and then handle the error. This code simply prints out the error, but you could present it to the user in an alert view.

If we do have a valid response, one easy thing to do with the response is to display the route on the map view. The route is an `MKPolyline`, which can be added to the map view as an overlay. You will also need to add a renderer for the overlay – this will turn the polyline into a graphic. Let's start by adding the route to the map:

```
let route = response.routes[0]
self.mapView.addOverlay(route.polyline)
```

The next step is to make sure that the map displays the route in its window. We'll also include some padding, so that the start and end of the route aren't right on the edges of the screen. The polyline has a bounding map rectangle property that you can use to set the visible map rectangle, along with the edge padding.

```
let padding = UIEdgeInsets(
  top: 40, left: 40, bottom: 40, right: 40)
self.mapView.setVisibleMapRect(
  route.polyline.boundingMapRect,
  edgePadding: padding,
  animated: true)
```

The last piece of the puzzle is the renderer for the map view overlays. You will need to implement the `MKMapViewDelegate` protocol in your `ViewController` class, as well as set the delegate on the map view to be the view controller, like this:

```
class ViewController: UIViewController, MKMapViewDelegate {
  @IBOutlet weak var mapView: MKMapView!

  override func viewDidLoad() {
    super.viewDidLoad()
    // Do any additional setup after loading the view.
    mapView.delegate = self
  }
}
```

To get the overlay to show up, use the mapView(_ mapView:, rendererFor overlay:) method in the MKMapViewDelegate protocol. This method returns an MKOverlayRenderer or one of its subclasses, such as MKPolylineRenderer:

```
func mapView(_ mapView: MKMapView, rendererFor overlay:
MKOverlay) -> MKOverlayRenderer {
  let renderer = MKPolylineRenderer(overlay: overlay)
  renderer.strokeColor = .red
  return renderer
}
```

Here, we simply create an MKPolylineRenderer for the overlay and then set the stroke color for the line to be red. There is no fill color for a polyline renderer, just stroke.

If we put the code to create the directions request into a function named getDirections() and then call that method from viewDidLoad(), we will end up with a class that looks like Listing 5-1.

Listing 5-1. Complete ViewController class for displaying a route

```
import UIKit
import MapKit

class ViewController: UIViewController, MKMapViewDelegate {
  @IBOutlet weak var mapView: MKMapView!

  override func viewDidLoad() {
    super.viewDidLoad()
    mapView.delegate = self
    getDirections()
  }

  func getDirections() {
    let request = MKDirections.Request()
    request.source = createMapItem(
      latitude: 40.7128, longitude: -74)
    request.destination = createMapItem(
      latitude: 38.91, longitude: -77.037)
    request.transportType = .automobile
    let directions = MKDirections(request: request)
    directions.calculate { (response, error) in
        guard let response = response else {
            print(error ?? "No error found")
            return
        }
        let route = response.routes[0]
        let padding = UIEdgeInsets(
          top: 40, left: 40, bottom: 40, right: 40)
        self.mapView.addOverlay(route.polyline)
        self.mapView.setVisibleMapRect(
          route.polyline.boundingMapRect,
```

```
        edgePadding: padding,
        animated: true)
  }
}

func createMapItem(latitude:Double, longitude:Double) ->
MKMapItem {
  let coord = CLLocationCoordinate2D(
    latitude: latitude,
     longitude: longitude)
  let placemark = MKPlacemark(coordinate: coord)
  return MKMapItem(placemark: placemark)
}

func mapView(_ mapView: MKMapView,
  rendererFor overlay: MKOverlay) ->
  MKOverlayRenderer {
  let renderer = MKPolylineRenderer(
    overlay: overlay)
  renderer.strokeColor = .red
  return renderer
  }
}
```

After running this application in the Simulator, you should expect to see a screen similar to Figure 5-1.

Figure 5-1. *Displaying driving directions as an overlay on a map view*

Understanding route steps

In addition to the route graphic that you can use as an overlay on the map view, the directions API will also return a set of steps for each route on the response. These steps are `MKRoute.Step` objects. Each route step is a single, discrete action that the user would take to follow the directions, such as walking down a street for 400 meters or driving down a road for 30 kilometers. All distances are given in meters, so you will probably want to convert to kilometers for longer distances or feet and miles for the United

States. Each step also includes the geometry associated with that step, so that you could overlay it on a map view. The properties on the MKRoute. Step class are

- polyline – The geometry for this route step
- instructions – The verbal directions to follow
- notice – Optional legal information or warnings associated with this step
- distance – The distance in meters
- transportType – One of the values from MKDirectionsTransportType (automobile, transit, walking)

If you wanted to simply iterate through each step in the route and print to console, you could use a function similar to this:

```
func printRouteSteps(_ route:MKRoute) {
  for step in route.steps {
    print("Go \(step.distance) meters")
    print(step.instructions)
  }
}
```

Let's take this a few steps further and build step-by-step directions into our application.

Building step-by-step directions

We'll modify the view controller we've already built, but you could certainly put step-by-step directions on its own screen. The first step we'll take will be to create the user interface elements for step-by-step directions:

- Previous and Next Step buttons to move between steps – These have black backgrounds, with white text for the normal state and light gray for the disabled state. Both should initially be disabled.

- An instructions label – This is multiple lines, to accommodate longer directions. It has a dark gray background with white text.

- A notice label – This label has a red background with white text, to separate it from the instructions label.

- A distance label – This label has a 0.8 alpha component, to give a little visual separation from the adjacent buttons.

Go ahead and add these user interface elements to the storyboard. You can arrange them however you like. You can also use Auto Layout to make sure the elements properly scale across all devices. The sample project for the book has the user interface elements at the bottom of the storyboard, with the buttons in line with the distance label, and the instructions label and notice label underneath that.

You should have something similar to Figure 5-2.

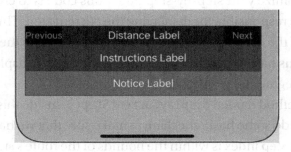

Figure 5-2. *The user interface elements for the step-by-step directions*

Create outlets for each user interface element, and use these names:

- `previousButton`
- `nextButton`
- `instructionsLabel`
- `noticeLabel`
- `distanceLabel`

Also create actions for both of the buttons, named `previous` and `next`. We will incorporate code into each of these methods to change the displayed step.

Last, add instance variables to the view controller to keep track of the current state. We will need to store the current route and the current step index. We will store the current route as an optional and initialize the current step index to zero:

```
var currentRoute:MKRoute?
var currentStepIndex = 0
```

Displaying the current step

One way to organize your step-by-step directions code is to create a function that is responsible for displaying the current step. This function will need to set the content of each label, disable or enable the previous and next buttons based on index, and update the map to display the current route segment.

Create a method named `displayCurrentStep()`. Inside this function, we are going to do some basic checking to make sure that we have a route, and the current step index is within the bounds of the route's steps array. The complete version of the `displayCurrentStep()` method is in Listing 5-2:

```
func displayCurrentStep() {
  guard let currentRoute = currentRoute else {
    return
  }
  if (currentStepIndex >= currentRoute.steps.count) {
    return
  }
}
```

Let's add some more functionality to this method. Continue to add these statements to displayCurrentStep(), after the checks. We'll keep track of the current step and then use that to set the properties of each of the labels:

```
let step = currentRoute.steps[currentStepIndex]
instructionsLabel.text = step.instructions
distanceLabel.text = "\(step.distance) meters"
```

We could add some functionality here for the distance label to change units if we wanted to. For the notice, not every route step will have a notice, so if there is not a notice (it is an optional), hide the notice label. Conversely, be sure to show the notice label if it is there:

```
if step.notice != nil {
    noticeLabel.isHidden = false
    noticeLabel.text = step.notice
} else {
    noticeLabel.isHidden = true
}
```

The next step is to manage the state of the buttons. The previous button should be disabled if the current step index is zero or less. The next button should be disabled if the current step index is the number of steps – 1 or more:

```
previousButton.isEnabled = currentStepIndex > 0
nextButton.isEnabled = currentStepIndex < (currentRoute.steps.
count - 1)
```

We still need to add the actions for each of these buttons, but let's finish out the step display by showing the polyline for the route step in the map view. Similar to what we did for the entire route, we are going to set the visible map rectangle based on the bounding map rectangle of the polyline. We'll also use the same padding on the edges to keep the segments visible. Add the following code to the end of your displayCurrentStep() method:

```
let padding = UIEdgeInsets(
  top: 40, left: 40, bottom: 40, right: 40)
mapView.setVisibleMapRect(
  step.polyline.boundingMapRect,
  edgePadding: padding,
  animated: true)
```

Now that we have all of the display code, we need two more pieces – saving the route in the completion handler for the directions API and the actions for the previous and next actions.

Saving the route in an instance variable

When we get the directions response from the API in the getDirections() method, we will need to store the route as an instance variable. Inside the completion handler, save the route to the currentRoute instance variable:

```
directions.calculate { (response, error) in
  guard let response = response else {
      print(error ?? "No error found")
      return
  }
  let route = response.routes[0]
  self.currentRoute = route
  self.displayCurrentStep()
  // Additional code follows
}
```

After the route has been saved, calling the displayCurrentStep() method we created in the previous section will initialize the step-by-step directions user interface with the current step.

Now, we need to add functionality to the actions for the previous and next buttons.

Actions for the previous and next buttons

The actions for the previous and next buttons will update the current step index. We will need to check that the current route is set first. We also then make sure that changing the step index stays within the bounds of the steps array.

For the previous() action, if the current step index is zero or less, the method will simply return:

```
@IBAction func previous(_ sender: Any) {
  if currentRoute == nil {
    return
  }
```

```
  if (currentStepIndex <= 0) {
    return
  }
  currentStepIndex -= 1
  displayCurrentStep()
}
```

The next() action is similar, except that the check is for whether the current step index is less than the number of steps – 1:

```
@IBAction func next(_ sender: Any) {
  guard let currentRoute = currentRoute else {
    return
  }
  if (currentStepIndex >=
    (currentRoute.steps.count - 1)) {
    return
  }
  currentStepIndex += 1
  displayCurrentStep()
}
```

After filling in the bodies for each of these actions, your application should be able to retrieve step-by-step directions. After running the application and clicking the Next button, you should see a screen like Figure 5-3.

Figure 5-3. *One step in the step-by-step directions*

The complete code for the view controller is in Listing 5-2, with all of the methods and instance variables.

Listing 5-2. ViewController class with step-by-step directions functionality

```
import UIKit
import MapKit

class ViewController: UIViewController, MKMapViewDelegate {
  @IBOutlet weak var mapView: MKMapView!
```

```swift
@IBOutlet weak var previousButton: UIButton!
@IBOutlet weak var nextButton: UIButton!
@IBOutlet weak var distanceLabel: UILabel!
@IBOutlet weak var instructionsLabel: UILabel!
@IBOutlet weak var noticeLabel: UILabel!

var currentRoute:MKRoute?
var currentStepIndex = 0

override func viewDidLoad() {
  super.viewDidLoad()
  // Do any additional setup after loading the view.
  mapView.delegate = self
  getDirections()
}

func getDirections() {
  let request = MKDirections.Request()
  // New York City
  request.source = createMapItem(latitude: 40.7128,
  longitude: -74)
  // Washington, DC
  request.destination = createMapItem(latitude: 38.91,
  longitude: -77.037)
  request.transportType = .automobile
  let directions = MKDirections(request: request)
  directions.calculate { (response, error) in
    guard let response = response else {
      print(error ?? "No error found")
      return
    }
    let route = response.routes[0]
    self.currentRoute = route
```

```
    self.displayCurrentStep()
    let padding = UIEdgeInsets(top: 40, left: 40, bottom: 40,
    right: 40)
    self.mapView.addOverlay(route.polyline)
    self.mapView.setVisibleMapRect(
      route.polyline.boundingMapRect,
      edgePadding: padding,
      animated: true)
  }
}

func displayRouteSteps(_ route:MKRoute) {
  for step in route.steps {
    print("Go \(step.distance) meters")
    print(step.instructions)
  }
}

func createMapItem(latitude:Double, longitude:Double) ->
MKMapItem {
  let coord = CLLocationCoordinate2D(latitude: latitude,
                      longitude: longitude)
  let placemark = MKPlacemark(coordinate: coord)
  return MKMapItem(placemark: placemark)
}

func mapView(_ mapView: MKMapView, rendererFor overlay:
MKOverlay) -> MKOverlayRenderer {
  let renderer = MKPolylineRenderer(overlay: overlay)
  renderer.strokeColor = .red
  return renderer
}
```

```
@IBAction func previous(_ sender: Any) {
  if currentRoute == nil {
    return
  }

  if (currentStepIndex <= 0) {
    return
  }
  currentStepIndex -= 1
  displayCurrentStep()
}

@IBAction func next(_ sender: Any) {
  guard let currentRoute = currentRoute else {
    return
  }
  if (currentStepIndex >= (currentRoute.steps.count - 1)) {
    return
  }
  currentStepIndex += 1
  displayCurrentStep()
}

func displayCurrentStep() {
  guard let currentRoute = currentRoute else {
    return
  }
  if (currentStepIndex >= currentRoute.steps.count) {
    return
  }
  let step = currentRoute.steps[currentStepIndex]
  instructionsLabel.text = step.instructions
  distanceLabel.text = "\(step.distance) meters"
```

```
  if step.notice != nil {
    noticeLabel.isHidden = false
    noticeLabel.text = step.notice
  } else {
    noticeLabel.isHidden = true
  }
  previousButton.isEnabled = currentStepIndex > 0
  nextButton.isEnabled = currentStepIndex < (currentRoute.
  steps.count - 1)
  let padding = UIEdgeInsets(top: 40, left: 40, bottom: 40,
  right: 40)
mapView.setVisibleMapRect(step.polyline.boundingMapRect,
  edgePadding: padding,
  animated: true)
  }
}
```

Next steps

There are some improvements to be made to this code – you could add a function that converts the distance to the correct units, or you could allow the user to switch between different transportation types (automobile, transit, or walking).

You could also combine this driving directions code with the local search from the previous chapter to allow users to choose where they want to go for directions.

Summary

Now that you have some experience with Apple's map directions, you can see how you might use this inside your own app, instead of sending the user to another application such as Apple Maps or Google Maps.

Chapter 6 switches focus away from maps, points of interest, and directions to geofencing. We will work with the region monitoring APIs in the `CoreLocation` framework to detect when a user enters or exits a given area, so that we can do something inside the app.

CHAPTER 6

Working with Geofences in CoreLocation

You can support region monitoring with geofences inside your iOS application with CoreLocation. iOS has built-in region monitoring, meaning that your application does not have to be in the foreground and also does not have to use excessive energy by continually checking the user's location.

Concepts for region monitoring

Conceptually speaking, region monitoring is simple. Your application can specify up to 20 geofences (called regions in CoreLocation). Each region gets a unique identifier, and you can specify whether or not the application is notified when the user enters or exits each region. The CoreLocation Manager (CLLocationManager) that we worked with in Chapter 2 can start and stop monitoring individual regions. You can also get a list of the currently monitored regions. Events for entering or exiting regions are delivered to the location manager delegate, which is typically a view controller or the app delegate class.

© Jeffrey Linwood 2020
J. Linwood, *Build Location Apps on iOS with Swift*,
https://doi.org/10.1007/978-1-4842-6083-8_6

The difficulties of region monitoring lie in the nuances for monitoring regions. For instance, region monitoring requires the always allow location permission, but the user will only be prompted to allow the when in use location permission the first time the application requests it. The always allow permission will occur in a separate request for the user when one of the geofences sends an enter or exit event to the application while it is running in the background.

The end user does not need to accept the always allow location permission for your application to monitor regions, but the triggers will only occur after the end user allows permission. This will require you to educate the user as to why they need to allow the application to have the always allow location permission.

In addition to permissions, your application will not be instantly notified when a user enters or exits a geofence. According to Apple, to avoid sending too many notifications to your application, iOS will require a 20-second wait and a minimum distance between when the region boundary was crossed and when your application will receive a notification. If your regions are small and the user is in a car, riding a bike, or even walking at a fast pace, they could be past the region by the time they get the alert.

Setting up your location-based application

This chapter will build on the discussion of the CoreLocation Manager from Chapter 2. We will need to initialize a location manager, set the delegate, and request permission to always get the user's location.

We will also need to set a message in the Info.plist file for each of two permissions:

- Privacy - Location When In Use Usage Description
  (NSLocationWhenInUseUsageDescription)

- Privacy - Location Always and When In Use Usage
  Description (NSLocationAlwaysAndWhenInUseUsage
  Description)

If you would like to know more about the location manager, delegate, and permissions, please see Chapter 2.

Create another Swift iOS project in Xcode with the Single View Application template. Name your application GeofencesApp. Next, change your ViewController class to match Listing 6-1.

Listing 6-1. Requesting always allow location authorization with CoreLocation

```
import UIKit
import CoreLocation

class ViewController: UIViewController {

    var locationManager:CLLocationManager!

    override func viewDidLoad() {
        super.viewDidLoad()
        locationManager = CLLocationManager.init()
        locationManager
            .requestAlwaysAuthorization ()
    }
}
```

We will also need to set the text for the permissions in the Info.plist file – we'll tell the user we are going to be monitoring geofences.

Open the Info.plist file in Xcode, and you will see the list of properties appear. Add entries for the two location privacy explanations (`NSLocationWhenInUseUsageDescription` and `NSLocationAlwaysAndWhenInUseUsageDescription`) as in Figure 6-1.

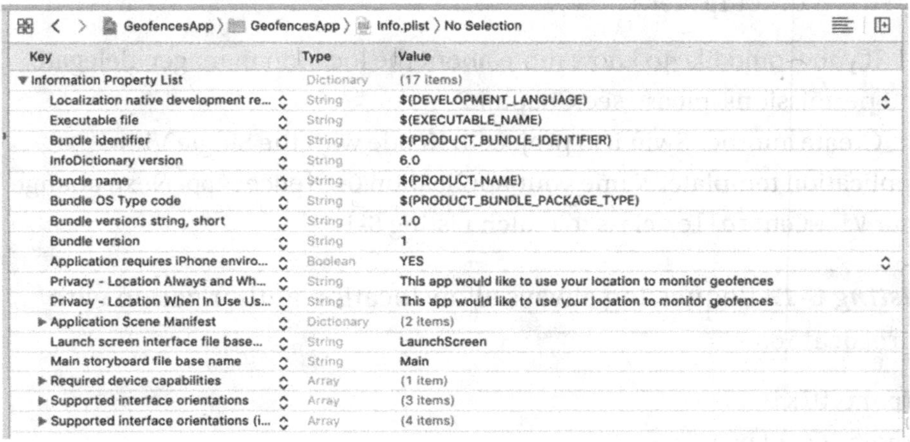

GeofencesApp 〉 GeofencesApp 〉 Info.plist 〉 No Selection

Key	Type	Value
▼ Information Property List	Dictionary	(17 items)
Localization native development re...	String	$(DEVELOPMENT_LANGUAGE)
Executable file	String	$(EXECUTABLE_NAME)
Bundle identifier	String	$(PRODUCT_BUNDLE_IDENTIFIER)
InfoDictionary version	String	6.0
Bundle name	String	$(PRODUCT_NAME)
Bundle OS Type code	String	$(PRODUCT_BUNDLE_PACKAGE_TYPE)
Bundle versions string, short	String	1.0
Bundle version	String	1
Application requires iPhone enviro...	Boolean	YES
Privacy - Location Always and Wh...	String	This app would like to use your location to monitor geofences
Privacy - Location When In Use Us...	String	This app would like to use your location to monitor geofences
▶ Application Scene Manifest	Dictionary	(2 items)
Launch screen interface file base...	String	LaunchScreen
Main storyboard file base name	String	Main
▶ Required device capabilities	Array	(1 item)
▶ Supported interface orientations	Array	(3 items)
▶ Supported interface orientations (i...	Array	(4 items)

***Figure 6-1.** Permission description for Always and When in Use Location Usage in the Info.plist file*

So far, these are all steps you would need to do for any iOS application that uses the user's location. Let's move on to creating geofences.

Getting started with region monitoring

The `CoreLocation` location manager is responsible for monitoring geofences, and your application is responsible for telling the manager which geofences to monitor. You can set geofences programmatically in your application, in case you need to retrieve them from a server, or let a user create their own geofences (for instance, for their home, school, and work locations).

The first step is to ensure that region monitoring is available for the region class you are using. In theory, any class that subclasses CLRegion could be used, but in practice, the only class that subclasses CLRegion in iOS 13 is CLCircularRegion, which draws a radius around a coordinate. The isMonitoringAvailable(for:) static method on the CLLocationManager takes a class as an argument, so you would typically pass in CLCircularRegion.self. If monitoring is available, you can create a region and then start monitoring it.

To create a circular region, you will need a CLLocationCoordinate2D center coordinate with a latitude and a longitude, a radius (in meters), and a unique string identifier. Using all of those to construct a CLCircularRegion will be similar to this:

```
let region = CLCircularRegion(center: coord, radius: 100,
identifier: "Geofence1")
```

Each region has two Boolean properties for triggers – notifyOnEntry and notifyOnExit. If both are set to false, the geofence won't do anything. Both may be set to true, or only one may be.

After instantiating and configuring the region, pass the region to an instance of the location manager with the startMonitoring(for:) method.

A complete Swift function that starts monitoring one geofence is in Listing 6-2 – add this to your ViewController class. You will want to modify the latitude and longitude in the geofence to your location.

Listing 6-2. Creating a geofence to monitor

```
func monitorGeofences() {
  if CLLocationManager.isMonitoringAvailable(for:
  CLCircularRegion.self) {
    let coord = CLLocationCoordinate2D(latitude: 37.5,
    longitude: -110.2)
```

```
    let region = CLCircularRegion(center: coord, radius: 100,
    identifier: "Geofence1")
    region.notifyOnEntry = true
    region.notifyOnExit = true

    locationManager.startMonitoring(for: region)
  }
}
```

As you can see in the preceding method, creating a region for a geofence and telling iOS to monitor it for entries and exits is pretty straightforward. The next part of this application will listen for changes in the user's location that will either take them into or out of the geofence.

Listening for geofence triggers

After registering geofences with the location manager, any entries or exits associated with that geofence will be sent to the location manager's delegate.

Start by modifying the viewDidLoad() method in the ViewController class to set the view controller as the location manager's delegate:

```
locationManager.delegate = self
```

The next step is to create an extension for the CLLocationManagerDelegate protocol at the end of the ViewController. swift source code file. Inside this extension, we are going to implement the locationManager(_ manager: didEnterRegion region:) and locationManager(_ manager: didExitRegion region:) methods.

A basic implementation of this extension is provided in Listing 6-3.

Listing 6-3. Listening to geofence triggers for entering and exiting regions

```
extension ViewController : CLLocationManagerDelegate {
  func locationManager(_ manager: CLLocationManager,
    didEnterRegion region: CLRegion) {
      print("Did enter \(region.identifier)")
  }

  func locationManager(_ manager: CLLocationManager,
    didExitRegion region: CLRegion) {
      print("Did exit \(region.identifier)")
  }
}
```

A more advanced usage of region monitoring might trigger business logic within the application, for instance, offering a discount, popping up a reminder from a to-do list, or offering to check you into a favored location. These would all be based on the region's identifier, which should be a unique string. For instance, you may want to use a primary id from a database or the id of an object retrieved from a RESTful resource on a server.

If you are starting monitoring a region that has the same identifier as another region, the existing region will be replaced. You can also monitor up to 20 regions at a time, so take that into account when considering your overall system design – you can't monitor any more than that with iOS.

You can test this code in the Simulator by changing the latitude and longitude of the simulated iPhone to match the geofence. Under the Features menu of the iOS Simulator, choose the Location submenu and then the Custom Location... menu item. The dialog box in Figure 6-2 will appear.

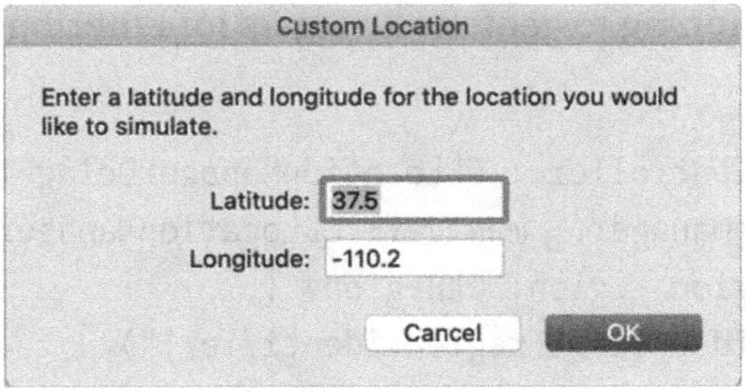

Figure 6-2. *Custom Location dialog box in the iOS Simulator*

You should see a message in the output window of Xcode that says "Did enter Geofence1". Change the Location of the simulator to "City Run" or another built-in location, and you will see a debug statement for leaving the Geofence.

Displaying a local notification inside the app

One very common use case for geofences is to display a local notification, even when the application is not active. To do this, you will typically add functionality to the AppDelegate class, although you can certainly encapsulate most of this into its own class, and then let the app delegate call into that class to perform the functionality.

When working with local notifications, you will need to ask the user for permission to display notifications (similar to the location permissions).

Setting up the notification center

Let's start by adding the imports we need to the AppDelegate class:

```
import CoreLocation
import UserNotifications
```

Once we have those, we can set up our user notification center in the `application(_ application: didFinishLaunchingWithOptions)` method of the app delegate with the following code:

```
UNUserNotificationCenter.current()
  .requestAuthorization(
    options: [.alert],
    completionHandler: {allowed, error in })
UNUserNotificationCenter.current().delegate = self
```

Here, all we are doing is requesting authorization from the user to display alerts for notifications. We could also request sound and badge access if we needed it by adding those to the options array. We do need to specify a completion handler, but it is OK if it is empty.

The next line sets the delegate for the user notification center. This is important for cases where the user enters or exits a geofence while the application is in the foreground. We will need to implement the `userNotificationCenter(_ center: willPresent notification: completionHandler)` method of the `UNUserNotificationCenterDelegate` delegate. Inside that method, we will only add one line, to handle the foreground notifications the same way we would as if the app were running in the background by displaying a notification alert. You could display an alert view here if you wanted.

To implement this notification center delegate, add an extension to the `AppDelegate` class, as shown in Listing 6-4.

Listing 6-4. The user notification center delegate extension for handling foreground notifications

```
extension AppDelegate: UNUserNotificationCenterDelegate {

  func userNotificationCenter(_
    center: UNUserNotificationCenter,
    willPresent notification: UNNotification,
```

```
    withCompletionHandler completionHandler:
      @escaping (UNNotificationPresentationOptions) -> Void) {
        completionHandler(.alert)
  }

}
```

This was a lot of boilerplate for a simple function, but it's essential if you want your local notifications to work properly when the app is in the foreground.

Displaying a local notification for a region

Our next step will be to write a function that creates a local notification from a monitored region. This function will take two arguments – a region and a Boolean for whether this is an enter or exit notification.

Inside this function, we will create a mutable notification content and set its title and body. We will also create a trigger that will display the notification a second after it is requested and a notification request that we will pass to the user notification center.

The following `displayNotification()` function in Listing 6-5 should be added to the `AppDelegate` class.

Listing 6-5. A function to display local notifications for a given monitored region

```
func displayNotification(_ region:CLRegion, isEnter:Bool) {
  let content = UNMutableNotificationContent()

  content.title = "Update for \(region.identifier)"
  content.body = isEnter ? "Did enter" : "Did exit"

  let trigger = UNTimeIntervalNotificationTrigger(
    timeInterval: 1,
    repeats: false)
```

```
let request = UNNotificationRequest(
    identifier: region.identifier,
    content: content,
    trigger: trigger)

UNUserNotificationCenter.current().add(request,
    withCompletionHandler: nil)
}
```

Now that we have a way to create notifications from regions, we just need to listen to region changes in the app delegate and then call this function.

Monitoring region changes in the app delegate

Inside the app delegate, we will need to create another instance of a CoreLocation location manager. These location managers all share the same set of regions, even if the region was added to the location manager in the ViewController class. Add the location manager as a constant property on the AppDelegate class:

```
let locationManager = CLLocationManager()
```

Inside the application(_ application: didFinishLaunching WithOptions) method, set the delegate of the location manager to self:

```
locationManager.delegate = self
```

Now we just need to implement the CLLocationManagerDelegate delegate as an extension in the AppDelegate.swift source code file, as shown in Listing 6-6. These two methods are identical to the ones we used earlier, in the basic region monitoring example. The difference is that instead of printing out a statement, the extension will call the displayNotification(_ region: didEnter:) method we wrote in the previous section.

Listing 6-6. CoreLocation location manager delegate that handles displaying notifications

```swift
extension AppDelegate : CLLocationManagerDelegate {

  func locationManager(_ manager: CLLocationManager,
    didEnterRegion region: CLRegion) {
      self.displayNotification(region, isEnter: true)
  }

  func locationManager(_ manager: CLLocationManager,
    didExitRegion region: CLRegion) {
      self.displayNotification(region, isEnter: false)
  }
}
```

Now run your application from the Simulator, and try entering and exiting the geofenced area with the Custom Location tools under the Features menu and Location submenu of the Simulator. You should see something similar to Figure 6-3.

Figure 6-3. *The iPhone Simulator displaying a local notification from a geofence*

You can continue to build on this example by implementing features to handle a user selecting a notification, either while the application is running or after the application has been terminated. Those are outside the scope of this book, with its focus on mapping and locations.

Removing geofences from the app

The location manager contains a set of geofences that are currently being monitored by the application. These regions are recreated every time the application loads and should be compared using the unique identifier, not an object comparison, as the instance may change between starting to monitor a region and retrieving a set of regions from the location manager. The name of the property of the location manager is `monitoredRegions`, and it consists of a set of `CLRegion` objects.

If you would like to stop monitoring all geofences, you can simply iterate through the set of regions and then call the `stopMonitoring(for:)` method on the location manager:

```
for region in locationManager.monitoredRegions {
  locationManager.stopMonitoring(for: region)
}
```

If you would like, you could compare the region's identifier to a known set of identifiers you would either like to keep monitoring or you would like to stop monitoring and remove the geofences then.

This wraps up our discussion of iOS region monitoring and geofences. This functionality is independent of any mapping technology used and can be used in both the foreground and background for iOS apps. The next chapter will show you how to use Google Maps for iOS, which is a similar technology to Apple's `MapKit` framework. You can certainly use these geofences in an application that uses Google Maps.

CHAPTER 7

Displaying a Map with the Google Maps SDK

Apple's `MapKit` framework isn't the only solution for mapping applications on iOS. Other providers offer mapping and routing technologies, including Google, Mapbox, Bing Maps by Microsoft, and ESRI's ArcGIS. In this chapter, as well as the following chapters, we are going to work with the Google Maps SDK for iOS. For applications on multiple platforms, you can use Google Maps on the Web, Android, and iOS. This can provide consistency across your application. You may also want to use imagery from Google in your map or use Google's driving directions or place information.

This chapter contains all of the steps needed to work with Google Maps in an iOS app. The following chapters will build on the project we create in this chapter.

Using the Google Maps Platform

Working with the Google Maps SDK is similar to working with Apple's `MapKit` framework, but there are a few differences. The first difference is that you will need to sign up with the Google Maps Platform. The second is that you will need to download the Google Maps library and integrate it into your Xcode project.

© Jeffrey Linwood 2020
J. Linwood, *Build Location Apps on iOS with Swift*,
https://doi.org/10.1007/978-1-4842-6083-8_7

Find out more about the Google Maps Platform at `https://cloud.google.com/maps-platform/`.

Google Maps has pricing and billing associated with its features, unlike Apple's Maps. At the time of writing (early 2020), Google offers $200/month (USD) of free credits for each user across Maps, Routes, and Places. In addition, at the time of writing, displaying maps inside a mobile application is free. These pricing offers could change at any time or be different outside the United States, so please check the pricing before signing up for the service.

Installing the Google Maps SDK for iOS library

Create a new iOS project in Xcode, named `GoogleMapsApp`, as a Single View Application with storyboards and Swift – similar to our other projects so far.

Google Maps for iOS has two different paths for installation. One way is to do a manual installation, following the step-by-step directions on the Google Maps installation page (`https://developers.google.com/maps/documentation/ios-sdk/start#step_2_install_the_sdk`). This is fairly involved and probably only worthwhile if you cannot use the second path, which uses the CocoaPods dependency manager.

CocoaPods is a dependency manager for iOS applications, similar to Homebrew for the Mac or Node Package Manager (NPM) for JavaScript. Instead of downloading libraries into your Xcode project and adding them manually, CocoaPods lets you declare which libraries your application uses, along with the versions, and then downloads and installs those libraries for you. This makes it much easier to upgrade frameworks and will help avoid issues where some libraries are incompatible with each other.

If you don't have CocoaPods installed on your system, it is distributed as a Ruby gem. You will need to install CocoaPods onto your Mac with this command:

```
sudo gem install cocoapods
```

Next, use the command line to navigate to the directory that contains your new Xcode project.

In that directory, type the following command to create a CocoaPods Podfile. Podfiles contain the dependencies for your project:

```
pod init
```

Now look in that directory, and view the Podfile that pod init just created. It should look something similar to Listing 7-1.

Listing 7-1. New CocoaPods Podfile for the Google Maps App

```
# Uncomment the next line to define a global platform for your
project
# platform :ios, '9.0'

target 'GoogleMapsApp' do
  # Comment the next line if you don't want to use dynamic
  frameworks
  use_frameworks!

  # Pods for GoogleMapsApp

end
```

So far, none of this has anything to do with Google Maps yet. We are going to add the GoogleMaps library as a dependency to our Podfile. Underneath the # Pods for GoogleMapsApp line, add the GoogleMaps pod. With the addition, your Podfile file should look like Listing 7-2.

Listing 7-2. CocoaPods Podfile with the GoogleMaps dependency

```
target 'GoogleMapsApp' do
  # Comment the next line if you don't want to use dynamic
  frameworks
  use_frameworks!

  # Pods for GoogleMapsApp
  pod 'GoogleMaps'
end
```

Now that the dependency is in place, CocoaPods can download the latest version of the Google Maps SDK for us and set it up in our iOS application.

Run the following command from the command line in the same directory that you ran pod init:

```
pod install
```

CocoaPods will install the GoogleMaps dependency, and it will also create an Xcode workspace for your application. This workspace will contain two targets – one for your application and one for the downloaded dependencies (called pods). You will need to open GoogleMapsApp.xcworkspace now, not GoogleMapsApp.xcodeproj, to build your application.

With CocoaPods you can pin the version of Google Maps to a specific version (at the time of writing, 3.7.0), using semantic versioning. See the CocoaPods documentation at https://cocoapods.org/ for more on how to use CocoaPods and Podfiles.

Go ahead and open the workspace in Xcode. Try running the iOS application (GoogleMapsApp) on the Simulator or on your device. You will not see anything but a blank white screen, but if there are any compilation errors or other issues, this is a good time to debug them. For the next step, we will set up the Google Maps API Key, so that we can start to use Google's Maps, Routing, and Places services.

Setting up a Google Maps API Key

Before we go any further, you will need a Google Maps API Key. Sign up at https://cloud.google.com/maps-platform.

When you enable the Google Maps Platform, check off the box for Maps, as shown in Figure 7-1.

Figure 7-1. *Enable the Google Maps Platform and select a product*

Click CONTINUE. On the next screen (Figure 7-2), create a new project named First Maps Project.

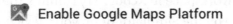 **Enable Google Maps Platform**

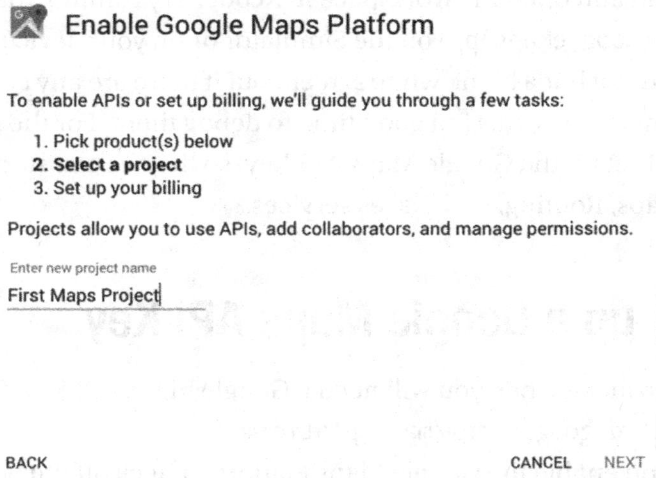

To enable APIs or set up billing, we'll guide you through a few tasks:

    1. Pick product(s) below
    2. Select a project
    3. Set up your billing

Projects allow you to use APIs, add collaborators, and manage permissions.

Enter new project name
First Maps Project

BACK   CANCEL   NEXT

Figure 7-2. *Create a new project for Google Cloud*

You will also need to set up a billing account for Google Maps, along with a credit card that Google can charge for usage over the free quota.

After that process, Google will ask if you want to enable the Google Maps Platform for your new project, as shown in Figure 7-3. Go ahead and click NEXT.

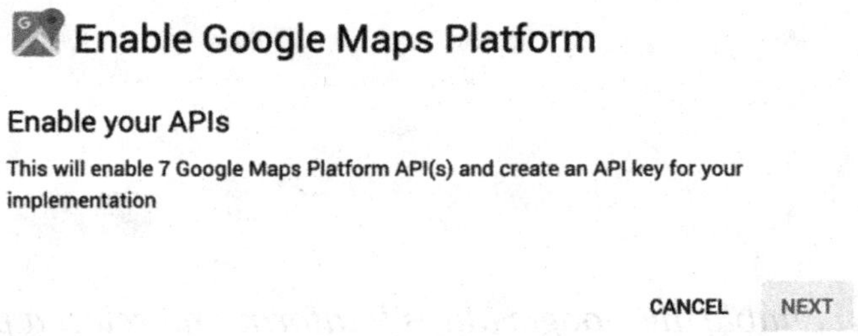

Enable Google Maps Platform

Enable your APIs

This will enable 7 Google Maps Platform API(s) and create an API key for your implementation

CANCEL   NEXT

Figure 7-3. *Enable Google Maps Platform APIs*

You will want to enable the Maps SDK for iOS – other platforms and services are available through the same interface.

If you are having trouble getting an API Key for the Maps SDK, there are alternative directions on Google's website: `https://developers.google.com/maps/documentation/ios-sdk/get-api-key`.

Last, you will want to create an API key. Under the APIs section of the web interface, find Maps SDK for iOS. Select the Credentials tab, and then click the link for Credentials in APIs & Services. On that screen, select the CREATE CREDENTIALS button, as shown in Figure 7-4, and then choose API key from the drop-down menu that appears.

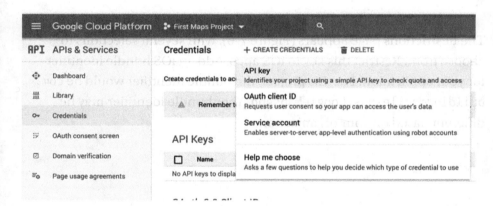

Figure 7-4. *Create Credentials for Google Maps Project*

The portal will create a new API Key for you, as seen in Figure 7-5. You will have access to this key in the future, so you do not need to save it right away. What you do need to do is to restrict usage of this key to just your application. This will keep others from using your API key in their projects, which would affect your billing.

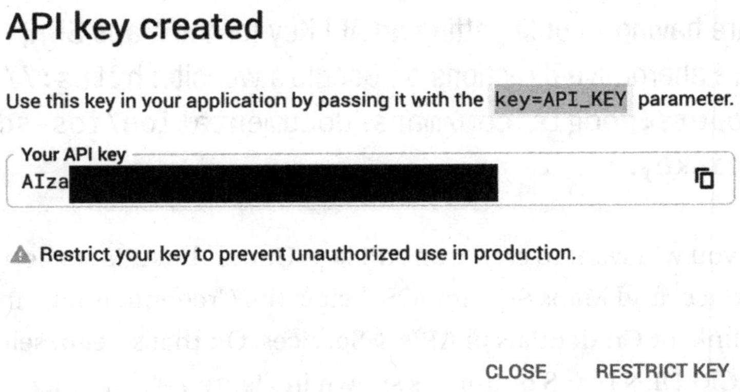

API key created

Use this key in your application by passing it with the `key=API_KEY` parameter.

Your API key
AIza██   ⬚

⚠ Restrict your key to prevent unauthorized use in production.

CLOSE   RESTRICT KEY

Figure 7-5. *The Google Maps API Key creation dialog box*

Choose the RESTRICT KEY button on the dialog box in Figure 7-5.
The Restrictions page appears (Figure 7-6), with several selections to
choose from. Restrict this key to iOS apps. Add an iOS bundle identifier
for your application. For this project, the bundle identifier would be com.
buildingmobileapps.GoogleMapsApp. Your bundle identifier may be
different based on your organization.

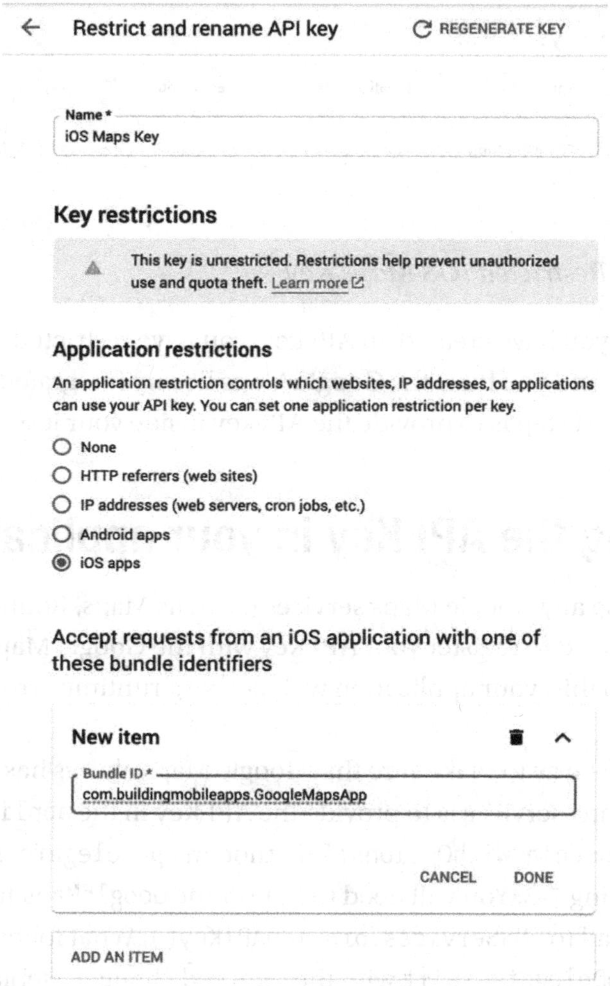

←   **Restrict and rename API key**   ⟳ REGENERATE KEY

Name *
iOS Maps Key

Key restrictions

⚠   This key is unrestricted. Restrictions help prevent unauthorized
use and quota theft. Learn more ⬈

Application restrictions

An application restriction controls which websites, IP addresses, or applications
can use your API key. You can set one application restriction per key.

○ None
○ HTTP referrers (web sites)
○ IP addresses (web servers, cron jobs, etc.)
○ Android apps
◉ iOS apps

**Accept requests from an iOS application with one of
these bundle identifiers**

New item   🗑   ∧

Bundle ID *
com.buildingmobileapps.GoogleMapsApp

CANCEL   DONE

ADD AN ITEM

Figure 7-6. *Restrict the use of a Google Maps API Key*

Be sure to press the DONE button after adding your bundle identifier
and then the Save button to persist your changes. After saving, you should
see that restriction appear next to your iOS key, as in Figure 7-7.

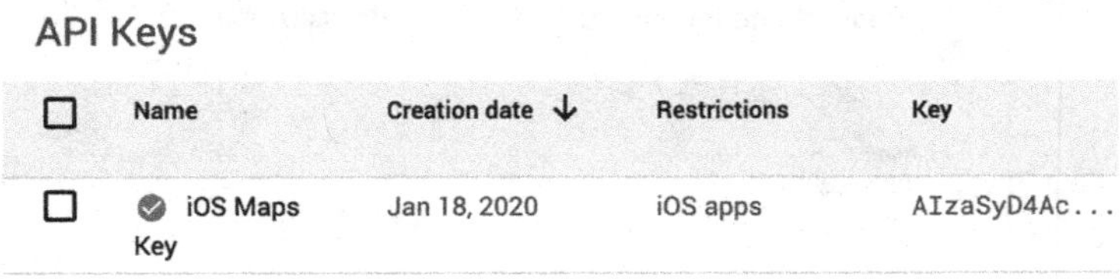

API Keys

	Name	Creation date ↓	Restrictions	Key
☐	✔ iOS Maps Key	Jan 18, 2020	iOS apps	AIzaSyD4Ac...

Figure 7-7. *Restricted iOS Maps Key*

Now that you have created an API key, you have restricted its use to your iOS app, and you have the Google Maps library integrated with your project, the next step is to provide the API key inside your iOS application.

Including the API Key in your application

Before you use any Google Maps services (such as Maps, Routing, or Places), you need to register your API Key with the Google Maps SDK. If you do not do this, your application will receive a runtime error from the SDK.

The easiest way to make sure that Google Maps always has the API key before using any services is to provide the API Key in the application(_ didFinishLaunchingWithOptions:) method in AppDelegate.swift, as shown in Listing 7-3. You will need to import the GoogleMaps framework and make a call to GMSServices.provideAPIKey(). What follows is a code listing for AppDelegate.swift with the required changes. Replace API-KEY with the API Key you created in the Google Cloud Console.

Listing 7-3. Partial version of AppDelegate.swift with Maps API Key

```
import UIKit

import GoogleMaps

@UIApplicationMain
```

```
class AppDelegate: UIResponder, UIApplicationDelegate {
    func application(_ application: UIApplication,
    didFinishLaunchingWithOptions launchOptions:
    [UIApplication.LaunchOptionsKey: Any]?) -> Bool {
        // Override point for customization after application
        launch.
        GMSServices.provideAPIKey("API-KEY")
        return true
    }
}
```

Now that you have an API key in place, it's time to move on to the fun part – displaying Google Maps within your app!

Displaying Google Maps with a map view

There are a couple of different ways we can add a map view (GMSMapView) to our iOS application. We can add it as a subview programmatically, we can add it to the storyboard as a UIView, and then change the custom class, or we can replace the view of the view controller with a map.

Displaying the map view on the storyboard is the easiest way. Simply drag a UIView onto the storyboard, and then change the custom class to be GMSMapView, as shown in Figure 7-8.

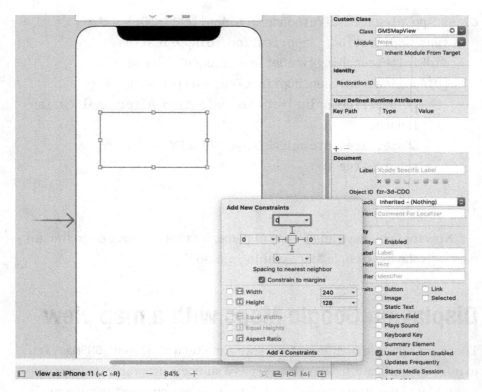

Figure 7-8. *Adding the Google map view to a storyboard*

Add constraints to the map view that it stretches from edge to edge (don't worry about the safe areas unless you want to). Now run the application in the Simulator – you should see a map like Figure 7-9 show up in your app!

Figure 7-9. *Basic Google Maps running in the Simulator*

Now, there is one final step for you to make this mapping application complete. Clicking or tapping the Google logo in the bottom left corner of the map needs to open up the Google Maps iOS app or the Google Chrome browser for iOS, if they are loaded onto the phone. If the end user doesn't have them, it will open up in Safari. We will need to allow our app to query for the proper URL schemes.

Allowing the Google Maps and Chrome URL schemes

The Google Maps SDK for iOS will attempt to open up either the Google Maps app or the Google Chrome app after someone taps on the Google logo in the lower left-hand corner of the map. The SDK will check to see if those apps are installed on the user's phone before opening them. The fallback is to open up the URL in Safari.

The first versions of iOS let any application check to see if any other application was installed on the phone. Unfortunately, this capability was abused, so Apple restricted the use of this permission. Any application bundle identifiers that you would like to check need to be specifically declared in the Info.plist file.

Add a row to the Info.plist. The key will be LSApplicationQueriesSchemes. There is not a corresponding entry in the drop-down that appears, so you will need to type the name in exactly. Change the type from String to Array. Now you can add any URL schemes that the app is going to query to the array. Here are the two for Google Maps and Google Chrome:

- comgooglemaps
- googlechromes

Your completed Info.plist file should look something similar to Figure 7-10.

▼ LSApplicationQueriesSchemes	⌄	Array	(2 items)
Item 0		String	comgooglemaps
Item 1		String	googlechromes
▶ Supported interface orientations (i...	⌄	Array	(4 items)

Figure 7-10. *The Info.plist file with the required URL query schemes*

Now that all of the required information is set up, we can move on to changing the way the map view displays information.

Changing display options on the map view

If we want to change display options on the map view, we will need to do so from code. Using the Assistant view in Xcode, create an outlet on your ViewController class for the Google map view, and name it mapView, as seen in Figure 7-11.

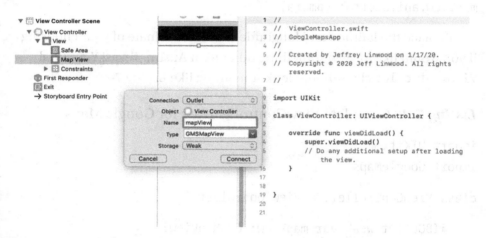

Figure 7-11. *Creating an outlet for the Google Maps map view*

The outlet property should look like this:

```
@IBOutlet weak var mapView: GMSMapView!
```

You will also need to add the import statement for the GoogleMaps framework to the top of the ViewController class:

```
import GoogleMaps
```

Now run your iOS application, just to make sure that nothing is broken. You should not see any changes yet. Let's go ahead and change the location of the map. Using Google Maps, we would create a camera position and then animate the map view to the new position. Add the following lines to your viewDidLoad() method:

```
let camera = GMSCameraPosition.camera(
  withLatitude: 30.25,
  longitude: -97.7,
  zoom: 7)
mapView.animate(to: camera)
```

Replace the latitude and longitude with a coordinate of your choosing if you would like to view something other than Austin, Texas! Your final ViewController class should look something like Listing 7-4.

Listing 7-4. Complete ViewController class for Google Maps

```
import UIKit
import GoogleMaps

class ViewController: UIViewController {

    @IBOutlet weak var mapView: GMSMapView!
    override func viewDidLoad() {
        super.viewDidLoad()
        // Do any additional setup after loading the view.
        let camera = GMSCameraPosition.camera(
          withLatitude: 30.25,
          longitude: -97.7,
          zoom: 7)
        mapView.animate(to: camera)
    }
}
```

Now that we have the basics for working with the Google Maps SDK on iOS, we can move on to more advanced topics, such as changing the type of map to satellite, terrain, or hybrid, adding map markers, or giving driving directions. We will reuse the Xcode project we built in this chapter to avoid having to repeat all of the setup and installation instructions.

CHAPTER 8

Exploring Google Map Views

In the previous chapter, we did all of the setup necessary to work with the Google Maps SDK for iOS. If you have not worked through Chapter 7, start there, as this chapter will pick up where that one left off.

In this chapter, we will explore the capabilities of the Google Maps map view. In particular, we will work with map types, map markers, and shapes.

Changing the type of map tiles

Get started by opening the application you built in Chapter 7. We are going to extend that project, so we do not have to repeat the setup process for Google Maps.

Google Maps comes with five different map types, which are specified in the GMSMapViewType enum:

- hybrid – Satellite tiles with labels

- none – No tiles, no labels

- normal – Default option, street map with labels

- satellite – The satellite tiles, but with no labels

- terrain – Useful for outdoor apps, has labels

© Jeffrey Linwood 2020
J. Linwood, *Build Location Apps on iOS with Swift*,
https://doi.org/10.1007/978-1-4842-6083-8_8

Setting the map type is straightforward – in the `viewDidLoad()` method of the `ViewController` class from Chapter 7, add one line at the bottom, as shown in Listing 8-1.

Listing 8-1. Changing the map type for Google Maps

```
override func viewDidLoad() {
  super.viewDidLoad()
  ...
  mapView.mapType = .terrain
}
```

You can always allow your users to set the map type themselves if you want to let them switch between satellite, terrain, and street map options. The map type can be changed at runtime without a problem.

Displaying map markers

Displaying a map marker on Google Maps is straightforward – simply create a map marker as a `GMSMarker` object, specify the position and title, and then tell the marker which map it belongs to.

This is a little different than `MapKit`, where you add a marker to a map directly. Create a new function in your `ViewController` class named `addMarker()`, with the code in Listing 8-2.

Listing 8-2. Adding a marker to the map

```
func addMarker() {
  let marker = GMSMarker()
  marker.title = "Austin"
  marker.snippet = "Texas"
```

```
marker.position = CLLocationCoordinate2D(
  latitude: 30.25, longitude: -97.75)
marker.map = mapView
}
```

Add a call to addMarker() in your viewDidLoad() method, and run
the application. You should see something similar to this after clicking the
map marker to display the info window. The info window in Figure 8-1 will
show the title and snippet properties, if they exist.

Figure 8-1. *Showing a map marker and info window on the map*

Changing the marker icon

By default, markers will show up as a red pin. The marker's `icon` and `iconView` properties control how the marker displays. The `icon` property takes a `UIImage` object. The `iconView` property takes a `UIView` object. The `iconView` property takes precedence over the `icon` property – if you set an `iconView`, the `icon` property will be ignored.

The `GMSMarker` class provides a helper function that creates a `UIImage` of the marker icon with the color that you specify (as a `UIColor`). This is helpful if you want to show markers with different colors on your map. To change the marker icon to blue, you would see something like this:

```
marker.icon = GMSMarker.markerImage(with: .blue)
```

You can pass any color in as an argument to the `markerImage()` method.

Responding to marker events

The `GMSMapViewDelegate` protocol contains many different callback methods you may end up using with your map application.

With respect to markers, the most common functionality you would implement would probably be to do something when a user taps on a marker or on an info window. Typically, if the marker has an info window, you would only do something if the user taps the info window, but it is possible to listen for taps on the marker, do something, and also still display the info window.

The first step would be to set the `delegate` property of the `mapView` to the view controller:

```
mapView.delegate = self
```

Next, create an extension of your `ViewController` class that implements the `GMSMapViewDelegate` protocol:

```
extension ViewController: GMSMapViewDelegate {

}
```

To do something when a user taps on an info window, implement the `mapView(_ didTapInfoWindowOf marker:)` method of the protocol:

```
func mapView(_ mapView: GMSMapView,
  didTapInfoWindowOf marker: GMSMarker) {
    print("Info: \(marker.title ?? "No Title")")
}
```

You have access to the map view, as well as the marker associated with that info window. If you need to do something when the user taps on an info window, implement the `mapView(_didTap marker:)` method. Return `true` if the map view does not need to process the default behavior for the tap (showing an info window) or `false` if the map view should proceed with the default behavior. The following code snippet returns false, so the map view will run this code and then display the info window:

```
func mapView(_ mapView: GMSMapView,
  didTap marker: GMSMarker) -> Bool {
    print("Marker: \(marker.title ?? "No Title")")
    return false
}
```

User data and markers

The preceding examples simply print out the marker's title, if there is one. Typically, you'd want to present a new view controller with details about the place represented by the selected marker. That requires some kind of way to link the selected marker object with an identifier or a data object.

The GMSMarker class has an optional userData property that can be used to store anything – strings, numbers, or your own objects. The Google Maps for iOS SDK will simply ignore it – your code is responsible for doing something with it. This makes passing in custom data very easy – if your map markers are showing City objects, for instance, simply set the user data property to the corresponding instance of the City class. You can also pass in an identifier, like an integer or a UUID, and then let your details view controller do the lookup from a data store.

We can try this out by adding user data to our marker in the addMarker() method:

```
marker.userData = 1234
```

If we then modify the mapView(_didTap marker:) method in our extension, we can see the user data printed out:

```
func mapView(_ mapView: GMSMapView,
  didTap marker: GMSMarker) -> Bool {
    print("Marker: \(marker.title ?? "No Title")")
    print(marker.userData ?? "No user data")
    return false
}
```

Again, you would probably use this to present a new view controller with more details about the marker, but this illustrates how you might retrieve this user data from the marker.

Adding shapes to the map

You may want to add lines, polygons, or circles to your map. For instance, if you had driving directions from one place to another, you might want to show the entire path on the map. You might also want to do a data visualization using circles on the map, for instance, to illustrate magnitude of earthquake shocks or the number of people living in a city or town.

Circles

Generally speaking, all of these work similarly, so let's start with the least complicated example – a circle. The GMSCircle class is like the GMSMarker class, in that you set its position with a latitude and longitude and then assign a map as a property. It differs from a marker because you have to set a radius that the circle covers on the map. This radius is in meters and corresponds to an actual geographic location. A marker would generally display at the same fixed size, no matter what zoom level you are at in the map. In addition to setting a radius, you also may set the fill color for the inside of the circle, the color used on the stroke outline of the circle, and the width of that outline.

The following code creates a light gray, semi-transparent circle over Austin, Texas, with a 20-kilometer radius and a dark gray outline:

```
func addCircle() {
  let circle = GMSCircle()
  circle.fillColor = UIColor(white: 0.6, alpha: 0.7)
  circle.strokeColor = .darkGray
  circle.radius = 20 * 1000
  circle.position = CLLocationCoordinate2D(
    latitude: 30.25, longitude: -97.75)
  circle.map = mapView
}
```

Make a call to addCircle() from your viewDidLoad() method, run your app, and you will see something similar to Figure 8-2 appear in the Xcode simulator.

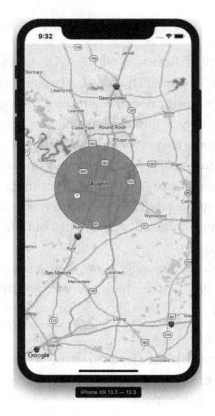

Figure 8-2. *Displaying a circle on the map*

Now that we've displayed a circle, let's move on to the next type of overlay, a polyline.

Polylines and paths

If you are showing a route or a path in your application, you can use polylines to display one line that consists of one or more different segments. With the Google Maps SDK for iOS, the way this works is that you construct a path as a GMSMutablePath object with two or more location coordinates, in the order that they will be connected. You then construct a

GMSPolyline object with that path. The path represents the data (latitudes and longitudes, as well as the order), and the polyline provides the rendering options for the map – line color and width. There is no fill color for the polyline with Google Maps – only a stroke color and a stroke width.

Start by creating a path:

```
let path = GMSMutablePath()
```

You can add CoreLocation coordinates or latitude and longitude pairs to the path. For this example, let's use latitude and longitude pairs to add several cities in Texas to the path. This path will have two segments:

```
path.addLatitude(30.25, longitude: -97.75)
path.addLatitude(29.4, longitude: -98.5)
path.addLatitude(29.76, longitude: -95.37)
```

Now that we have a path with two or more coordinates, we can construct a polyline with the path:

```
let polyline = GMSPolyline(path: path)
```

You can set the display options for the polyline by defining a new stroke color and stroke width:

```
polyline.strokeColor = .red
polyline.strokeWidth = 3
```

Last, you do need to remember to tell the polyline which map to display on:

```
polyline.map = mapView
```

Here are all of these statements combined into one function:

```
func addPolyline() {
  let path = GMSMutablePath()
  path.addLatitude(30.25, longitude: -97.75)
```

```
    path.addLatitude(29.4, longitude: -98.5)
    path.addLatitude(29.76, longitude: -95.37)
    let polyline = GMSPolyline(path: path)
    polyline.strokeColor = .red
    polyline.strokeWidth = 3
    polyline.map = mapView
}
```

If you were to call that function from your app, it would look similar to Figure 8-3.

Figure 8-3. *Displaying a polyline from a path of latitude and longitude pairs*

Typically, you would probably construct the path in a loop, reading from a database, the JSON response of an API call, or some other data structure. If you are working with the Google Directions API, you can create the path from the encoded path that a valid route returns. We'll build a driving directions application that uses the Google Directions API and Google Maps in the next chapter.

Polygons

Polygons are similar to polylines, in that you construct them with a path of coordinates. The difference is that polygons will draw an additional line between the last coordinate and the first coordinate, completing the outline of the shape. In addition, similar to circles, you can set a fill color on a polygon. Here is an example of a polygon drawn using the same coordinates as the polyline earlier:

```
func addPolygon() {
  let path = GMSMutablePath()
  path.addLatitude(30.25, longitude: -97.75)
  path.addLatitude(29.4, longitude: -98.5)
  path.addLatitude(29.76, longitude: -95.37)
  let polygon = GMSPolygon(path: path)
  polygon.strokeColor = .black
  polygon.strokeWidth = 2
  polygon.fillColor = UIColor(
      red: 1, green: 0, blue: 0, alpha: 0.3)
  polygon.map = mapView
}
```

The only differences between the preceding code and the polyline code are using the GMSPolygon class instead of GMSPolyline and being able to specify a fill color.

Call the `addPolygon()` method at the end of your `viewDidLoad()` method, and you should see a triangle appear, like the one in Figure 8-4.

Figure 8-4. *Displaying a polygon on the map*

Now that you've seen how to draw shapes on the map, it's time to discuss how to remove shapes after they are no longer needed.

Removing markers and shapes

Each marker or shape has a `map` property that points to the map view they display on. If you would like to clear a marker or shape from the map, simply set the `map` property to `nil`:

```
mapMarker.map = nil
```

This is useful for removing individual markers or shapes or different groups of markers or shapes. If you're processing search results and then displaying them on the map, you may want to clear all previous results off of the map before displaying the new results. To clear all markers and shapes off of the map and only display the map tiles, use the `clear()` method on the map view:

```
mapView.clear()
```

You can now create any new markers or shapes that you need.

Conclusion

In this chapter, we discussed how to change the map tiles used in your map view, using the `mapType` property of the map view. We also added markers to our map and learned how to change the marker icon. When a user taps on a marker or info window, we also learned how to handle those events and how to pass custom data on a marker that we could use. Last, we looked at adding circles, polylines, and polygons and then how to remove markers and shapes.

In the next chapter, we build on our discussion of polylines and paths to provide driving directions from Google Directions API on a map view.

CHAPTER 9

Using Directions with the Google Directions API

The Google Directions API is a simple HTTPS API that lets you get driving directions to a destination. The Google Directions API does not have a native Swift implementation from Google – instead, you make an HTTPS API call to Google and parse the JSON results in the response. Part of a successful response is a path that can be turned into a polyline and displayed on the map.

This chapter builds on the work done in Chapters 7 and 8. In Chapter 7, we set up a basic iOS application project using CocoaPods with the Google Maps API. In Chapter 8, we discussed how to display shapes and markers on the map. For this chapter, we are going to reuse the same project as Chapters 7 and 8 – or you can create a new project that uses the Google Maps iOS SDK and has a map view on the storyboard.

We will need to do a little more work to enable the Google Directions API and create a new API key to use with the HTTP API.

© Jeffrey Linwood 2020
J. Linwood, *Build Location Apps on iOS with Swift*,
https://doi.org/10.1007/978-1-4842-6083-8_9

Setting up the Google Directions API

In Chapter 7, we created an API Key and enabled the Google Maps APIs.
Because we only chose to enable maps, we need to add the Google
Directions API to our Google Cloud Project. Log in to your account at
`https://cloud.google.com/maps-platform`.

Select APIs from the menu in the sidebar (Figure 9-1).

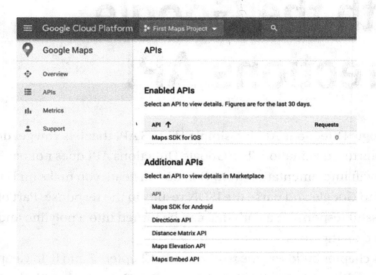

Figure 9-1. *Enabled APIs and Additional APIs for Google Maps*

You will see the APIs you added for Google Maps here, along with a list
of additional APIs you could use in your project. Under Additional APIs,
you will find the Google Directions API (Figure 9-2).

Figure 9-2. *Enabling the Google Directions API*

Enable the Directions API here.

Caution   If you forget to enable the Google Directions API, when you make an HTTP request, you will get an error message similar to this: **"This API project is not authorized to use this API."**

After enabling the Directions API, you will need to create a new API key. Visit the Credentials screen for Google Cloud Platform's APIs and Services at https://console.cloud.google.com/apis/credentials. You should see your iOS Maps Key, as in Figure 9-3.

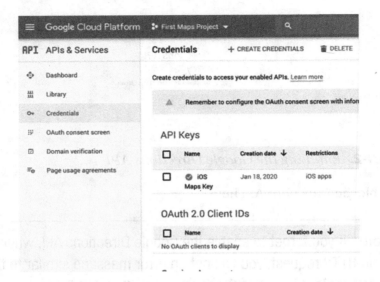

Figure 9-3. *Credentials screen for creating API keys*

Create a new credential, and when the drop-down menu appears, choose API Key. A new API key will be generated, but it will be unrestricted – the next step is to restrict the API key.

Restricting the API Key

Choose the RESTRICT KEY button on the dialog box that appears (Figure 9-4).

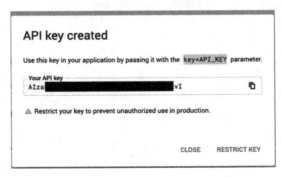

Figure 9-4. *API key created dialog box, with RESTRICT KEY button*

Although it may seem like you want to restrict the Google Directions API Key to an iOS app, that doesn't work with making an HTTPS call to the Google Directions API. If you are going to directly embed the API Key into an iOS app, you need to choose None for application restrictions.

The best practice for this is not to embed the API Key into the app, like we do with the sample project – this works for prototyping and development, but means that if someone can look for static strings in your app, they could extract the string.

You also want to be careful if you upload this project into a public Git repository as open source. It's very easy to get an API key if it's published, even if you go back later and make a commit that takes it out.

Instead, what you can do is make a web service that proxies the request from your application to Google. Your web service can be the only code that knows about your API key, and it can live on an application server or in a serverless cloud environment as a function. Put the API Key into an environment or context variable, rather than directly embedding it in the code, or in a configuration file.

You can control access to this web service or function by requiring a valid user credential, if your app has typical user signup and authentication.

This also has the advantage of not breaking existing mobile applications if you need to rotate your Google API keys – you can simply set a new environment variable for your web service or cloud function and then restart your service or function.

For this project, we can put those concerns aside, so that we can try out the Google Directions API. Just don't upload this source code to your public Git repository, or if you do by accident, delete the API Key from Google Cloud Platform.

Under API restrictions, restrict this key to the Google Directions API, and then save the changes, as shown in Figure 9-5.

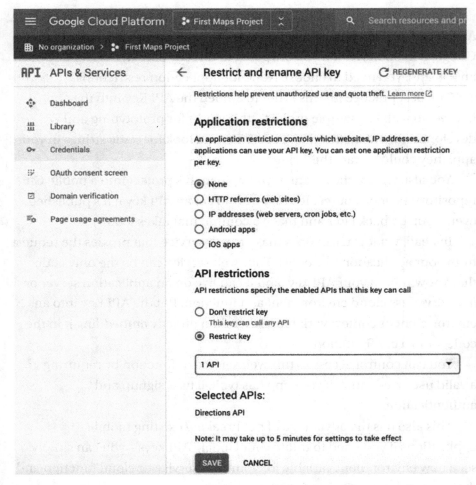

Figure 9-5. *Restrict API key screen*

Once you have saved the Google Directions API key, make note of it.

Using the Google Directions API

Unfortunately, there is not an official helper library for iOS or Swift from Google for the Google Directions API. Instead, we can use the standard iOS networking library to make the API calls. The Google Directions API consists of an HTTPS endpoint that takes request parameters and returns a JSON response (there is also an XML endpoint).

To implement this API in Swift, we can use the URLSession class (and its related classes) to make the HTTPS call. We can either parse the JSON into dictionaries and arrays using the JSONSerialization class or define a data structure that implements the Codable protocol for the JSON response and use the JSONDecoder class. The second approach is much cleaner, as the first approach requires copious uses of if let and guard let statements with the nested structure of the Google Directions API response. We create a basic set of Swift structures to hold the Directions API response in this chapter.

Creating the URL

The Google Directions API is an HTTPS-based API, and you can easily test your requests out in a web browser. You will need to declare a constant to hold an API Key that supports the Google Directions API. We set this API up in the first part of this chapter. The following value is an example API key; substitute yours in its place:

```
let apiKey = "AIzaZZZZZZZZZZZZZZZZZ"
```

You will also need to build up the URL for the API call. There are many different parameters you can send to the Google Directions API. The following three parameters are required:

- origin – A street address, set of coordinates, or a Google Places ID

- destination – Same as origin

- key – A valid API Key

Other parameters you may include are

- mode – Driving (default), walking, bicycling, transit

- waypoints – Intermediate destinations for the route, except for transit

- alternatives – True/false; will return multiple routes if they are available, and no intermediate waypoints are specified

- avoid – Tolls, highways, ferries, indoor; which methods of transportation to avoid in the calculated routes

In addition to the preceding parameters, others you may want to consider are transit_routing_preference, language, arrival_time, departure_time, region, units, and traffic_model. See the detailed explanations of each of these parameters at the Google Directions API documentation page (https://developers.google.com/maps/documentation/directions/intro).

An example Google Maps Directions URL might look like the following, with the API key being interpolated into the string:

```
let directionsUri = "https://maps.googleapis.com/maps/api/
directions/json?origin=Austin,TX&destination=Houston,TX&key=\
(apiKey)"
```

You can certainly use your own location or an interesting place as either the origin or destination.

Calling the Directions API with URLSession

We need to make the call to the Google directions API ourselves. Using the standard URLSession and its related classes, we will create a data task and then call another method to process the response as a Data object.

The following `retrieveDirections()` method only handles the networking aspect, not the data processing. Add the method in Listing 9-1 to your `ViewController` class. You could also extend this method to take arguments for the origin and destination, if you wanted to ask the user for those through a text field, or perhaps use the user's current location as a latitude/longitude pair.

Listing 9-1. Making an HTTPS call to the Google Directions API

```
func retrieveDirections() {

  let directionsUri = "https://maps.googleapis.com/maps/api/
  directions/json?origin=Austin,TX&destination=Houston,TX&key=\
  (apiKey)"
  let session = URLSession(configuration: .default)
  guard let url = URL(string: directionsUri) else {
    print("Could not parse directions URI into URL")
    return
  }
  let task = session.dataTask(with: url) { (data, response,
  error) in
    guard let data = data else {
      print("Error returning data from url")
      print(error?.localizedDescription ?? "No error defined")
      return
    }
    self.processDirections(data)
  }
  task.resume()
}
```

The next step is to process the `Data` object that we get from the HTTPS call and turn it into usable data structures.

Processing the directions response

Our request to the Google Directions API asks for a JSON response. We could also ask for XML, but that is harder to parse. With JSON, we need to decode the Data object using the JSONDecoder. We will define a set of data structures based on the JSON response from the Google Directions API.

An entire JSON response from the Google Directions API is too long to include in this chapter, but you can make an HTTPS request in your web browser to inspect the complete response. An edited version of the JSON response follows in Listing 9-2, with ... marking the removed parts. Most notably, the geocoded waypoints have been trimmed, the encoded paths for the polylines have been trimmed, and the number of steps in the route has been reduced to one.

Listing 9-2. Trimmed JSON response from Google Directions API

```
{
  "geocoded_waypoints": [
    ...
  ],
  "routes": [
    {
      "bounds": {
        "northeast": {
          "lat": 30.2671031,
          "lng": -95.3657891
        },
        "southwest": {
          "lat": 29.69176959999999,
          "lng": -97.7506595
        }
      },
```

```
"copyrights": "Map data ©2020 Google, INEGI",
"legs": [
  {
    "distance": {
      "text": "165 mi",
      "value": 265936
    },
    "duration": {
      "text": "2 hours 33 mins",
      "value": 9172
    },
    "end_address": "Houston, TX, USA",
    "end_location": {
      "lat": 29.76043,
      "lng": -95.3698084
    },
    "start_address": "Austin, TX, USA",
    "start_location": {
      "lat": 30.2671031,
      "lng": -97.74307949999999
    },
    "steps": [
      {
        "distance": {
          "text": "0.5 mi",
          "value": 776
        },
        "duration": {
          "text": "3 mins",
          "value": 167
        },
```

```
                "end_location": {
                    "lat": 30.2649534,
                    "lng": -97.73539049999999
                },
                "html_instructions": "Head <b>east</b>...",
                "polyline": {
                    "points": ...
                },
                "start_location": {
                    "lat": 30.2671031,
                    "lng": -97.74307949999999
                },
                "travel_mode": "DRIVING"
            },
            ...
        ],
        "traffic_speed_entry": [ ],
        "via_waypoint": [ ]
    }
    ],
    "overview_polyline": {
        "points": ...
    },
    "summary": "TX-71 E and I-10 E",
    "warnings": [ ],
    "waypoint_order": [ ]
    }
    ],
    "status": "OK"
}
```

Inspecting this JSON response, we can determine which fields are useful for our application and which can be ignored. For instance, we may be building a hiking application, so we could ignore the traffic field. We will also create the bounding box from the polyline path, so we don't need to parse it out separately.

Let's start with a few basic data structures for the response, as seen in Listing 9-3, so that we can display the overview of the route on the map. We are only going to get the route and the points in the overview polyline. Define these structures in your ViewController.swift file for easy reference.

We are using Codable here for easy serialization between JSON and data structures. Otherwise, we would have to parse the nested response as a series of dictionaries and arrays, and the resulting Swift code would not be very maintainable.

Listing 9-3. Data structures for the Google Directions API response

```
struct GoogleDirectionsResponse:Codable {
  var routes:[Route]?
}

struct Route:Codable {
  var overview_polyline:OverviewPolyline?
}

struct OverviewPolyline:Codable {
  var points:String?
}
```

Once we have the data structures defined, we can decode the Data object from the HTTPS response (Listing 9-4). We do need to use a do-try-catch statement for this process, so that we can handle any JSON decoding errors or mismatches between our defined data structures and the response (such as a missing required property).

Last, once we have the response parsed out, we check to see if there are any points in the response for the overview, and if so, pass them to a separate method to display them. That method will execute on the main thread, as it changes the user interface.

Listing 9-4. Decoding the JSON response into a data structure

```
func processDirections(_ data:Data) {
  let decoder = JSONDecoder()
  do {
    let response = try decoder.decode(GoogleDirectionsResponse.
    self, from: data)
    print(response)
    guard let points = response.routes?.first?.overview_
    polyline?.points else {
      return
    }
    // displaying the polyline on the map has to be on the main
       thread
    DispatchQueue.main.async {
      self.displayOverviewPolyline(points)
    }
  }
  catch let error as NSError {
    print("JSON Error: \(error)")
  }
}
```

Add the method in Listing 9-4 to your `ViewController` class. We still need to write the `displayOverviewPolyline()` method to show the user which way the route goes.

Displaying the route as a polyline

The response from the Google Directions API includes the points in the route as an encoded string that can be turned into a GMSPath object. This path object represents all of the points on the route, which includes the beginning and ends of all of the segments. You can use a path to create a polyline and then configure that polyline with the appropriate stroke color and width.

You also need to set the map property on the polyline to the Google map view. We also store the polyline as a member variable on the view controller at the end of the function (Listing 9-5).

Add the polyline as a member variable on the ViewController class:

```
var routePolyline: GMSPolyline?
```

For more about polylines and paths, see Chapter 8.

Listing 9-5. Displaying the Google Directions API response as a polyline on Google Maps

```
func displayOverviewPolyline(_ points:String) {
  guard let routePath = GMSPath(
    fromEncodedPath: points) else {
    return
  }
  let polyline = GMSPolyline(path: routePath)
  polyline.strokeColor = .red
  polyline.strokeWidth = 3
  polyline.map = mapView
  self.routePolyline = polyline
  updateMapBounds(routePath)
}
```

As a quick reminder, this method needs to be called on the main thread, just like any other user interface modification.

At the end of the method, we included a call to a method that updates the map bounding box, based on the path the route takes.

Updating the map bounding box

The GMSCoordinateBounds class is used to create a bounding box that you can then use with a camera update to display a rectangular segment of the world in the map view. You can create one of these bounds with a GMSPath object, like the list of points used in the route overview. That bounds will have no additional padding, but the camera update allows you to specify padding as a UIEdgeInsets structure.

Putting this together with a call to the moveCamera() method on the map view, we get the following function (Listing 9-6), which you can add to your ViewController class.

Listing 9-6. Displaying the entire route in the map view

```
func updateMapBounds(_ routePath: GMSPath) {
  let bounds = GMSCoordinateBounds(path: routePath)
  let insets = UIEdgeInsets(top: 100, left: 100, bottom: 100,
              right: 100)
  let cameraUpdate = GMSCameraUpdate.fit(bounds, with: insets)
  mapView.moveCamera(cameraUpdate)
}
```

You could adjust those edge insets as you like, to give the route enough padding. Having it stretch across the whole screen can look strange.

Now that all of the functions are complete, try running your application in the Simulator. You should see a red line appear on the Google Map for your route, like the following figure. Double-check the API key for your driving directions if you have problems (you can always test the URL in a web browser).

Figure 9-6. *Displaying Google directions on a Google Map*

This completes our use of the Google Directions API for this project. The next step to building out your application would probably be to add turn-by-turn directions, by breaking the route down into its different legs and steps.

Next steps: Displaying each leg and step

To extend this project out, we would need to add additional data structures to our project to decode each leg of the route, as well as each step of each leg. You could also add previous and next buttons that would walk up and down the list of steps, showing the HTML instructions and displaying the step polyline on the map.

Last, when you are done with this project, go back into the Google Cloud Platform console at `https://console.cloud.google.com/` and delete your Google Directions API key. It's always a good idea to clean up your project credentials!

In Chapter 10, we will use the Google Places SDK for iOS to search for points of interest and display them on a Google map. You could combine the work we did in this chapter with the search functionality in Chapter 10 to build some interesting applications on your own!

CHAPTER 10

Using Google Places in Your iOS App

Google Places provides a rich database of locations and photos to iOS apps through the Google Places SDK. With the SDK, your mobile app can augment its location abilities with additional details and photos or even provide a places search with autocomplete.

We are going to build on the discussion in Chapter 7 about CocoaPods and using Google APIs in your mobile app. In particular, getting a Google Places API key is similar to getting an API key for the Google Directions API or the Google Maps API.

Google Places is on a pay-per-use billing model, with billing credits that should cover usage in development and testing. Please check the Google Maps Platform billing website (https://developers.google.com/maps/billing/gmp-billing) for the latest information. Also, you will find more details there about what usage costs and how changing the fields in a place request affects pricing.

Building a places finder with a map

Our project in this chapter will be to create a search interface for businesses in the Google Places database, based on the currently visible region in a Google Maps map view. We are going to start with the Google

© Jeffrey Linwood 2020
J. Linwood, *Build Location Apps on iOS with Swift*,
https://doi.org/10.1007/978-1-4842-6083-8_10

Places autocomplete view controller first and then add the Google Maps marker at the end of the chapter.

This project demonstrates how to search for places by name in Google Places with autocomplete, as well as how to integrate the Google Places SDK for iOS into your project. We will use the full-screen autocomplete search view controller for Google Places, which makes adding this functionality pretty simple.

Creating the project

Create a new Single View Application in Xcode, using Swift. Choose storyboard as the user interface framework. Name the app `PlacesApp`. The example project for this chapter uses `com.buildingmobileapps` as the organization identifier, making the app's bundle identifier `com.buildingmobileapps.PlacesApp`. We'll use this bundle identifier in the next section of this chapter, when we create an API key and restrict it for use.

Getting a Google Places API key

Similar to the previous chapter with the Google Directions API, or Chapter 7 with the Google Maps API, you will need to get a Google Places API key. You need to go to the Google Cloud Console, which can be found at this URL, `https://console.cloud.google.com`, and then enable the Google Places API for your project.

You will also need to create a new API key. Start by going to the Credentials screen, which is in found in the Google Cloud Platform menu under the APIs & Services section (Figure 10-1).

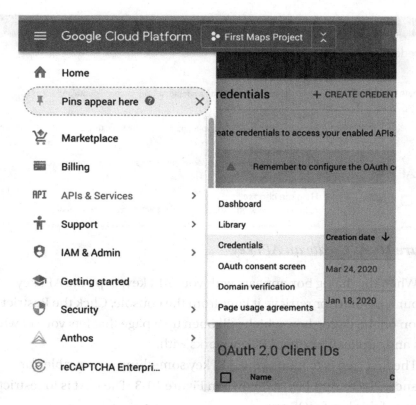

Figure 10-1. *Credentials location in APIs & Services menu*

Click the CREATE CREDENTIALS button, and choose API key
(Figure 10-2).

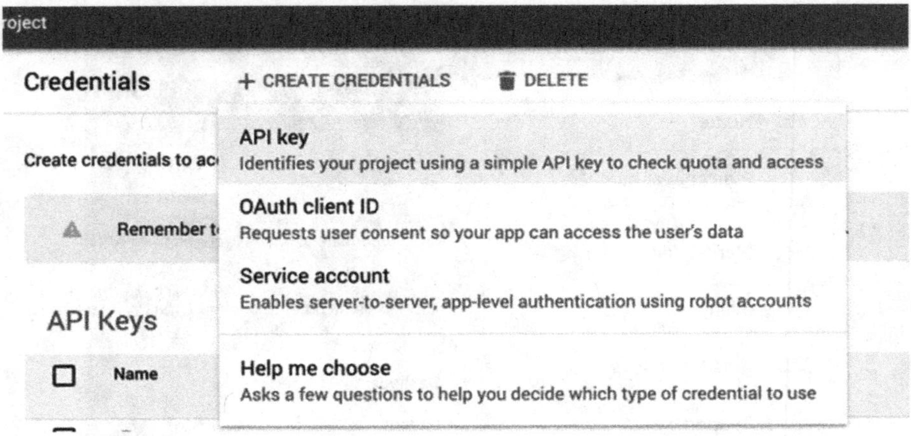

Figure 10-2. *Create an API key*

When the dialog box appears with your API key, copy the API key to your clipboard, or retrieve it later from the console. Click the Restrict button on the dialog box, which will open up a page that lets you set which APIs and applications this API key works with.

The first step is to name your API key something memorable, for instance, Places App Key, as shown in Figure 10-3. The next is to restrict the use of this key to iOS apps.

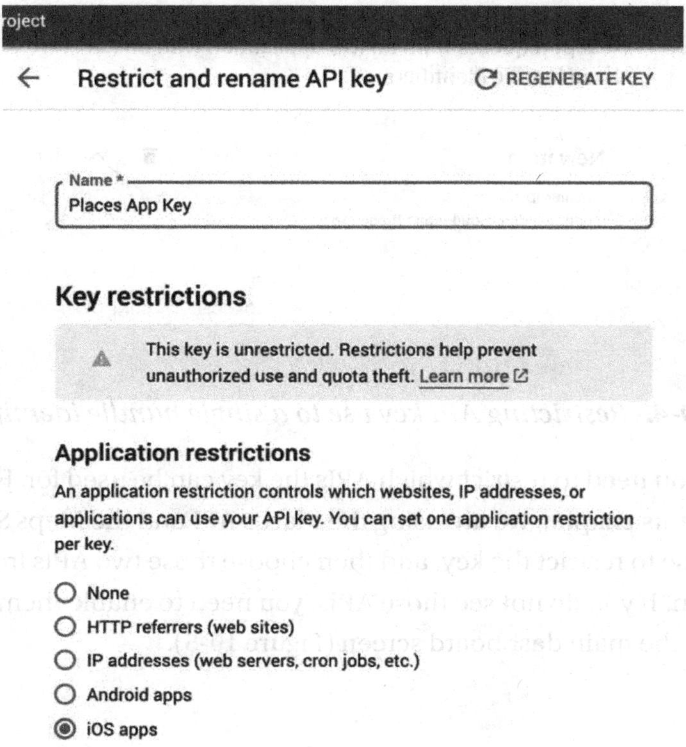

Figure 10-3. *Naming the API key and restricting to iOS apps*

After choosing iOS apps, you will see a place to enter in your app's bundle identifier. Go ahead and put in your app's bundle identifier, and then click the DONE button underneath the text field (Figure 10-4).

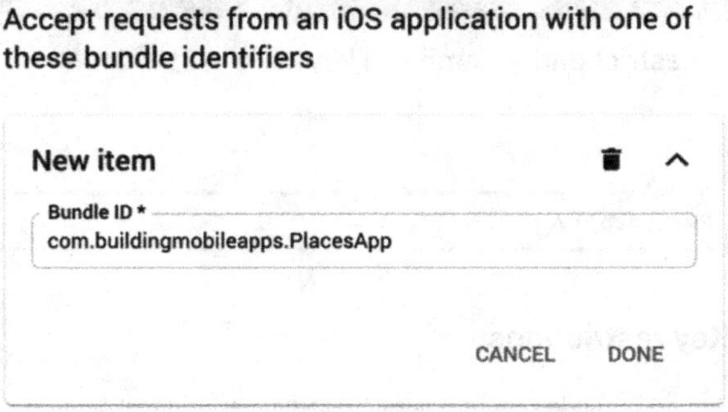

Accept requests from an iOS application with one of these bundle identifiers

New item   🗑 ∧

Bundle ID *
com.buildingmobileapps.PlacesApp

CANCEL   DONE

Figure 10-4. *Restricting API key use to a single bundle identifier*

Last, you need to restrict which APIs the key can be used for. For the project in this chapter, we are using the Places API and the Maps SDK for iOS. Choose to restrict the key, and then choose those two APIs from the drop-down. If you do not see those APIs, you need to enable them for your project on the main dashboard screen (Figure 10-5).

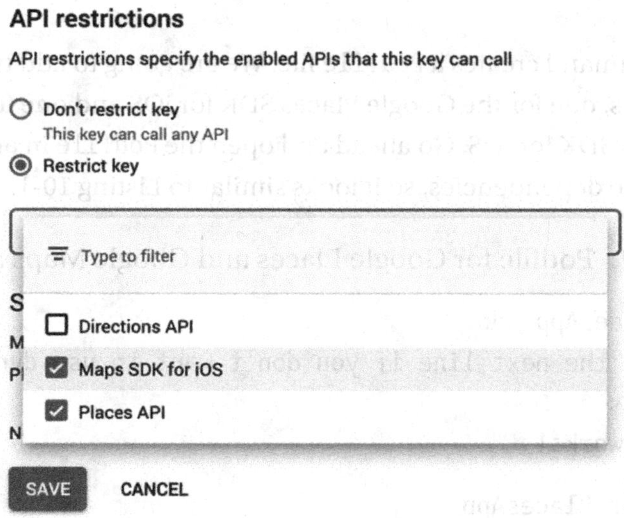

API restrictions

API restrictions specify the enabled APIs that this key can call

○ Don't restrict key
This key can call any API

◉ Restrict key

≡ Type to filter

☐ Directions API

☑ Maps SDK for iOS

☑ Places API

SAVE   CANCEL

Figure 10-5. *Restricting API key use to two APIs*

Save those changes, and then the console will return to the API keys screen. We will use the API key in the app shortly, so leave the page open. You can always go back into the console and retrieve your API keys, however, unlike some vendors that only provide a secret authorization token once.

Our next step is to include the Google Places SDK and the Google Maps SDK in our app project with CocoaPods.

Setting up CocoaPods

If you are new to CocoaPods, see the discussion in Chapter 7 on how to install it on your Mac. We are going to follow a similar process to get our app project set up. The first step is to open up the Terminal app on your Mac and change directories to the directory that has our project. Then, create a Podfile for your project with this command:

```
pod init
```

That command creates a `Podfile` file. We are going to add two dependencies, one for the Google Places SDK for iOS and one for the Google Maps SDK for iOS. Go ahead and open the `Podfile` in an editor, and add these dependencies, so it looks similar to Listing 10-1.

Listing 10-1. Podfile for Google Places and Google Maps SDKs

```
target 'PlacesApp' do
  # Comment the next line if you don't want to use dynamic
  frameworks
  use_frameworks!

  # Pods for PlacesApp
  pod 'GooglePlaces', '3.8.0'
  pod 'GoogleMaps', '3.8.0'
end
```

After editing your Podfile, run the following command to install your dependencies, and then create an Xcode workspace:

```
pod install
```

Now, only use the `PlacesApp.xcworkspace` file with Xcode, not the `PlacesApp.xcodeproj` file, or the CocoaPods dependencies won't be included in the build.

Open the `PlacesApp.xcworkspace` file in Xcode, and we can get started building the app!

Providing an API key for Google Places and Google Maps

The next step to building our project is to specify API keys for the Google Places SDK for iOS, as well as the Google Maps SDK for iOS. We can use the same API key for each, as we enabled support for both APIs in the first part of this chapter. For Google Places, the GMSPlacesClient class has a static method named provideAPIKey() that you use before calling anything else in the Google Places SDK. Similarly, we will call the provideAPIKey() method on the GMSServices class for Google Maps. Add the GooglePlaces framework and the GoogleMaps frameworks as import statements in the AppDelegate class. We will provide the API keys for both of the Google SDKs in the app delegate's application(_:didFinishLaunchingWithOptions:) method.

Listing 10-2 is a selection from the AppDelegate class, missing some boilerplate methods that we did not modify. Replace the value of the apiKey constant with the API key you created earlier in this chapter.

Listing 10-2. Selection from the AppDelegate class

```
import UIKit
import GooglePlaces
import GoogleMaps

@UIApplicationMain
class AppDelegate: UIResponder, UIApplicationDelegate {

    func application(_ application: UIApplication,
    didFinishLaunchingWithOptions launchOptions:
    [UIApplication.LaunchOptionsKey: Any]?) -> Bool {
```

```
    let apiKey = "AIza..."
    GMSPlacesClient.provideAPIKey(apiKey)
    GMSServices.provideAPIKey(apiKey)
    return true
  }
}
```

Now that you have the Google Places and Maps SDKs set up, let's use it to add some functionality to our project!

Creating the user interface

Your view controller needs two user interface elements – a Google Maps map view and a button to Find Businesses in the map area. Using the storyboard (Figure 10-6), you can drag a UIView and a UIButton onto the main view for your ViewController class. Change the identity of the UIView class to GMSMapView, to make it a Google Maps map view. Add constraints to the map view to have it fill all available space in the view, and then add constraints to the button to anchor it to the bottom of the screen. Change the button's text to say Find Businesses, and choose any colors or fonts that you like to make it stand out against the map.

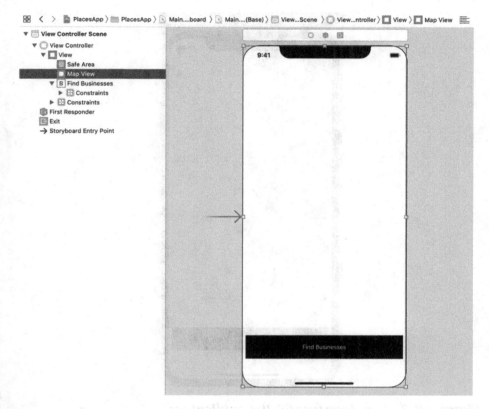

Figure 10-6. *Storyboard showing map view and button*

One thing to note: the button can't be a child view of the map view; it has to be a child view of the main `UIView` for the `ViewController` screen.

After running your project, if everything is set up correctly, your project will look similar to Figure 10-7.

Figure 10-7. *User interface for the application*

You could also create the map view and the button programmatically, if you wish.

Create an outlet named `mapView` for the Google Maps map view, using the Assistant view in Xcode:

```
@IBOutlet weak var mapView: GMSMapView!
```

Next, create an action named `findBusinesses` for the button. You should have something similar to this action in your `ViewController` class:

```
@IBAction func findBusinesses(_ sender: Any) {

}
```

That concludes our work with the storyboard. The next part of the project will be to display the Google Places autocomplete view controller when a user taps on the button.

Understanding the autocomplete search

When you add some kind of places search to your project, you will want to include autocomplete – forcing users to type in the exact name as specified in the database won't be successful. The Places SDK for iOS includes user interface elements for autocomplete, as well as a way to make autocomplete queries programmatically, so that you can implement your own user interface.

Two modern user interface elements are included in the Places SDK. The first is a stand-alone full-screen view controller that handles text search as well as displaying results. The other user interface element is a search results view controller that works with a search bar that you implement. For this chapter, we will work with the stand-alone view controller, but the concepts for the search are similar between the two different user interfaces.

The basic steps for configuring and displaying an autocomplete full-screen view controller are

- Create an instance of the GMSAutocompleteViewController class.

- Give geographic boundaries for the place search.

- Decide which data fields you need back from the query.

- Filter the results by type of place (city, street address, establishment).

- Display the view controller.

- Implement the delegate for callbacks when search is completed or canceled by user.

Let's go through each of these steps in more detail, as we build out the places search functionality in our project.

Creating the autocomplete view controller

To start out our places search project, we will need to create an instance of the GMSAutocompleteViewController class. We'll also need to set a delegate for the autocomplete view controller, and we will create an extension later in this chapter to handle these delegate methods. Go ahead and assign the autocomplete view controller's delegate to self for now:

```
let vc = GMSAutocompleteViewController()
vc.delegate = self
```

All of the code snippets in this and the following sections will go into the action named findBusinesses() we created earlier. This function can be found printed out in full in Listing 10-3, which is after the discussion of each individual step.

Setting geographic boundaries for the search

We can tell Google Places what geographic area to search for places using the autocomplete search. You can either use this area as a preference, so that results within this geographic space get boosted up toward the top of the list, or as a restriction, where places outside of this geographic area won't be shown at all, even if they are nearby.

With our project, we are going to use the visible region from the Google map view as our boundary. That region needs to be transformed into a GMSCoordinateBounds object, which you can do with the GMSCoordinateBounds constructor:

```
let region = mapView.projection.visibleRegion()
let bounds = GMSCoordinateBounds.init(region: region)
vc.autocompleteBounds = bounds
```

We will also restrict our results to only those found within the geographic bounds:

```
vc.autocompleteBoundsMode = .restrict
```

You do not have to be this restrictive – instead you can bias results toward those found in the map, but if a user is looking for something specific, and it happens to be close to the map but not in it, it will still return as a result. This is the default behavior for the autocomplete search. If you would like to use it, do not set the autocompleteBoundsMode parameter, or set it to the .bias value.

You also do not have to use any geographic bounds, in which case you would simply omit setting the autocompleteBounds property. You could also construct the geographic bounds yourself, for instance, if you were building a place search for a given region or city.

The next step is to determine which data fields your view controller needs to fetch from the Google Places API.

Requesting a subset of data fields

The Google Places API will return all data fields by default for autocomplete, including premium ones such as reviews that cost extra. As you probably do not need all fields, you can set a specific set of fields that you do need in your result.

To construct the list of fields, you will need to combine a set of GMSPlaceField enum values together with an OR (|) operator. The following is a list of several of these fields that you could use for your application:

- coordinate
- formattedAddress
- name

- openingHours

- phoneNumber

- photos

- placeID

- rating

- website

For our purposes, we are going to stick to the basic place details and simply request the name, place ID, and coordinate. We will use these later to create a marker on the map.

Our code will combine the raw values from the enum values as unsigned integers and then construct a GMSPlaceField value from that. We also return from the function if the GMSPlaceField constructor fails to create an object. This particular API could have been made a little easier to use, for instance, by taking a set of values instead. We also need to set the placeFields property of the autocomplete view controller:

```
// needed for the map marker
let fields = UInt(GMSPlaceField.name.rawValue) |
  UInt(GMSPlaceField.placeID.rawValue) |
  UInt(GMSPlaceField.coordinate.rawValue)

guard let placeFields = GMSPlaceField(rawValue: fields) else {
  return
}

vc.placeFields = placeFields
```

Not to be confused with the fields, we now need to tell Google Places what type of search results we want.

Filtering results by type

The autocomplete view controller supports different types of places for search results. The supported types, as well as a no filter option, are all available on the GMSPlacesAutocompleteTypeFilter enum. The options are

- noFilter
- address
- city
- establishment
- geocode
- region
- city

To use one of these options with the autocomplete view controller, you need to create a GMSAutocompleteFilter instance and then set the filter's type property. On the autocomplete view controller, you will need to set the autocompleteFilter property with your filter object:

```
let filter = GMSAutocompleteFilter()
filter.type = .establishment
vc.autocompleteFilter = filter
```

We used the establishment type, but you could certainly use one of the other filters. Try them out to see what type of results they give back in your area.

Displaying the view controller

The autocomplete view controller expects to be full screen, so you can present it as a modal from your view controller, as seen in Figure 10-8:

```
present(vc, animated: true, completion: nil)
```

If you like, you could create the autocomplete view controller in one method and then display it from another method. For this project, we combined these two into one method for simplicity.

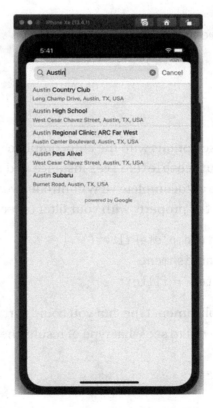

Figure 10-8. *Displaying the autocomplete view controller for Google Places*

The complete findBusinesses() method, with all of the preceding steps, is listed in Listing 10-3.

Listing 10-3. Displaying autocomplete view controller for Google Places search

```
@IBAction func findBusinesses(_ sender: Any) {
  let vc = GMSAutocompleteViewController()
  vc.delegate = self

  // search for places in this area
  let region = mapView.projection.visibleRegion()
  let bounds = GMSCoordinateBounds.init(region: region)
  vc.autocompleteBounds = bounds

  // only return results visible on the map
  vc.autocompleteBoundsMode = .restrict

  // needed for the map marker
  let fields = UInt(GMSPlaceField.name.rawValue) |
    UInt(GMSPlaceField.placeID.rawValue) |
    UInt(GMSPlaceField.coordinate.rawValue)

  guard let placeFields = GMSPlaceField(rawValue: fields) else {
    return
  }

  // only return asked for fields
  vc.placeFields = placeFields

  // we are looking for businesses/points of interest
  let filter = GMSAutocompleteFilter()
  filter.type = .establishment
  vc.autocompleteFilter = filter
```

```
// display as modal
present(vc, animated: true, completion: nil)
}
```

When the user chooses a place from the list or they decide to cancel, your view controller will need to dismiss the autocomplete view controller. We will discuss that in the next section about implementing the delegate methods for the autocomplete search.

Implementing the delegate for autocomplete

With the GMSAutocompleteResultsViewControllerDelegate protocol, your application will get notified when certain events happen with the autocomplete view controller. We are going to implement several methods from this delegate as an extension to our ViewController class.

In particular, the functions called when a user selects a place, when a user cancels the search request, or when an unrecoverable error occurs are required. The optional methods inform the delegate that an autocomplete request has been made, an autocomplete request has been updated, and a user has chosen a value from the list (but the API has not been called to get the place details yet).

Add an extension to your ViewController class for the GMSAutocompleteResultsViewControllerDelegate protocol:

```
extension ViewController: GMSAutocompleteViewControllerDelegate {

}
```

If you try to compile your project at this point, Xcode will inform you that the protocol has required methods and will offer to create stubs for the three required methods. You can let Xcode do that or copy the definitions from Listing 10-4.

Let's start by dismissing the autocomplete view controller in all three methods, as we see in Listing 10-4. Add these functions to your extension.

Listing 10-4. Implementing methods in the autocomplete view controller delegate

```
func viewController(_ viewController:
  GMSAutocompleteViewController,
      didAutocompleteWith place: GMSPlace) {
  viewController.dismiss(animated: true,
                        completion: nil)
}

func viewController(_ viewController:
  GMSAutocompleteViewController,
      didFailAutocompleteWithError error: Error) {
  viewController.dismiss(animated: true,
                        completion: nil)
}

func wasCancelled(_ viewController:
    GMSAutocompleteViewController) {
    viewController.dismiss(animated: true,
                        completion: nil)
}
```

Next, let's add some functionality to the first method, when a user selects a place. We will print out the place details, with the fields we requested from the Google Places API. If there are any required third-party attributions, we will also print those.

When you work with places returned from the Google Places API, some of those places may have attributions that you are required to display. Those come back on the GMSPlace object as the attributions property. For more on Google's current policy for attributions, see this web page: https://developers.google.com/places/ios-sdk/attributions.

Our updated method will look similar to this:

```
func viewController(_ viewController:
  GMSAutocompleteViewController,
     didAutocompleteWith place: GMSPlace) {
  viewController.dismiss(animated: true,
                        completion: nil)
  print(place)
  print(place.attributions ?? "No attributions")
}
```

Displaying the place on the map

If you are going to display Google Places data on a map, it must be a Google map, not an iOS MapKit map or a map from another provider. You can display places data outside of a map, but you need to display the Powered by Google image found at the attributions web page: https://developers.google.com/places/ios-sdk/attributions.

We are going to display the selected place on the map as a map marker. Start by adding a new function to your ViewController class named addMarker. This function will take a GMSPlace object as an argument named place:

```
func addMarker(_ place:GMSPlace) {
}
```

Now call that `addMarker` method at the end of the first method in the autocomplete view controller delegate extension, after printing out the place details:

```
print(place)
print(place.attributions ?? "No attributions")
addMarker(place)
```

We discussed how to add map markers to Google Maps in Chapter 8. We'll use the place fields we requested from the Google Places API to populate the marker and then display it on the map, as you can see with the code in Listing 10-5.

Listing 10-5. Displaying a place from the Google Places SDK on a Google map

```
func addMarker(_ place:GMSPlace) {
  let marker = GMSMarker()
  marker.position = place.coordinate
  marker.title = place.name
  marker.icon = GMSMarker.markerImage(with: .blue)
  marker.userData = place
  marker.map = mapView
}
```

When you run the project, you should see a Google map appear. Zoom or scroll on the map to find the location you want to search for places, and then tap the Find Businesses button. You will see the autocomplete view controller appear. When you select one of those places, you will see a blue marker appear on the map. Tapping the marker makes the name from the Google Places API appear, as you can see in Figure 10-9.

Figure 10-9. *Showing a map marker in Google maps for a Google Places place*

We put the GMSPlace object into the userData property on the map marker so that we could have access to the data in the place later. For instance, you could extend this application to retrieve photos for the place when a user taps on the marker.

Additional functionality in Places SDK

There is a lot of additional functionality in the Google Places SDK for iOS that we did not cover in this chapter. We only discussed the full-screen view controller for autocomplete search and not how to implement a custom user interface for search. We also did not cover how to request place details for a given place id, which we could use to get more data fields from the API.

In addition, you can also translate the user's current location into a place, letting you tell the user where they are. With the information in the photos data field for a place, you can retrieve photos, if there are any in Google Places.

This chapter concludes our discussion of Google's Map Platform and its components for iOS. In the next chapter, we will learn how to get started with Mapbox, another mapping provider.

CHAPTER 11

Getting Started with the Mapbox SDK

In this chapter, we will set up and use Mapbox maps in an iOS app. Mapbox is an independent mapping data provider that publishes software development kits for iOS, Android, and the Web. Mapbox allows you to easily style your maps, so that you can give your application a custom look and feel. We will work with map styles in the next chapter.

The example application we build in this chapter is similar to the introductory applications we built with Apple's `MapKit` and Google Maps.

Getting a Mapbox access token

You will need an access token to use Mapbox services, so you will need to create an account at `www.mapbox.com`. While you are creating an account, also take some time to understand Mapbox's pricing and free tier limits. At the time of writing, you can utilize Mapbox at the free level for up to 25,000 monthly active users on mobile devices, with payment being required for numbers of users above that amount. This could certainly change, so make sure that Mapbox fits the needs you have and your budget before building it into your application.

Once you create a Mapbox account and review the pricing, you will need to create an access token to use in your Mapbox application.

© Jeffrey Linwood 2020
J. Linwood, *Build Location Apps on iOS with Swift*,
https://doi.org/10.1007/978-1-4842-6083-8_11

Although you could use a default access token, it's better to create an access token for each of your Mapbox projects, in case you need to revoke a token or limit its capabilities. Find the Create a token button (Figure 11-1) on your Mapbox account page.

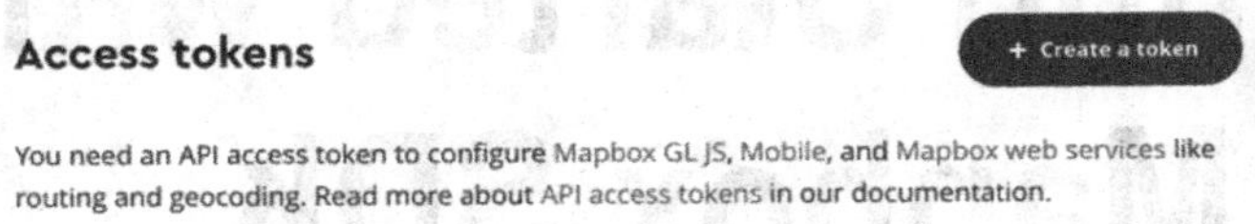

Access tokens

+ Create a token

You need an API access token to configure Mapbox GL JS, Mobile, and Mapbox web services like routing and geocoding. Read more about API access tokens in our documentation.

Figure 11-1. *The Create a token button*

Click the Create a token button, and name your access token FirstMapboxApp (or anything else you choose) on the next screen (Figure 11-2). The defaults are fine for the token scopes.

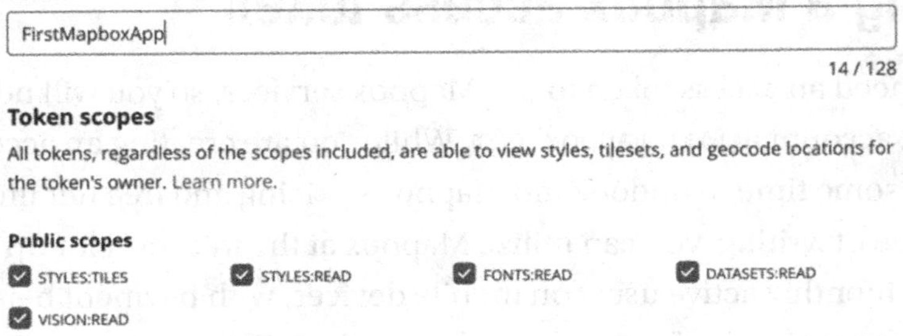

‹ Back to all access tokens

Create an access token

Token name
Choose a name to help associate it with a project.

Name

FirstMapboxApp

14 / 128

Token scopes
All tokens, regardless of the scopes included, are able to view styles, tilesets, and geocode locations for the token's owner. Learn more.

Public scopes

☑ STYLES:TILES   ☑ STYLES:READ   ☑ FONTS:READ   ☑ DATASETS:READ
☑ VISION:READ

Figure 11-2. *Creating an access token*

Create your token (at the bottom of the Create an access token screen), and then confirm your password if the web application prompts you. You will be taken to a list of your access tokens. Keep your access token confidential, and don't share it publicly, such as in a source code repository. We will add this access token to our application's `Info.plist` file after we set up our Xcode project.

Now that we have our access token, let's create an Xcode project and add the Mapbox SDK for iOS.

Starting a new project with the Mapbox SDK

We are going to build a new iOS application to demonstrate Mapbox functionality. Create a new project in Xcode, named `FirstMapboxApp`. This project should be a Single View Application, use Swift as the programming language, and use storyboard/UIKit for the user interface, as seen in Figure 11-3.

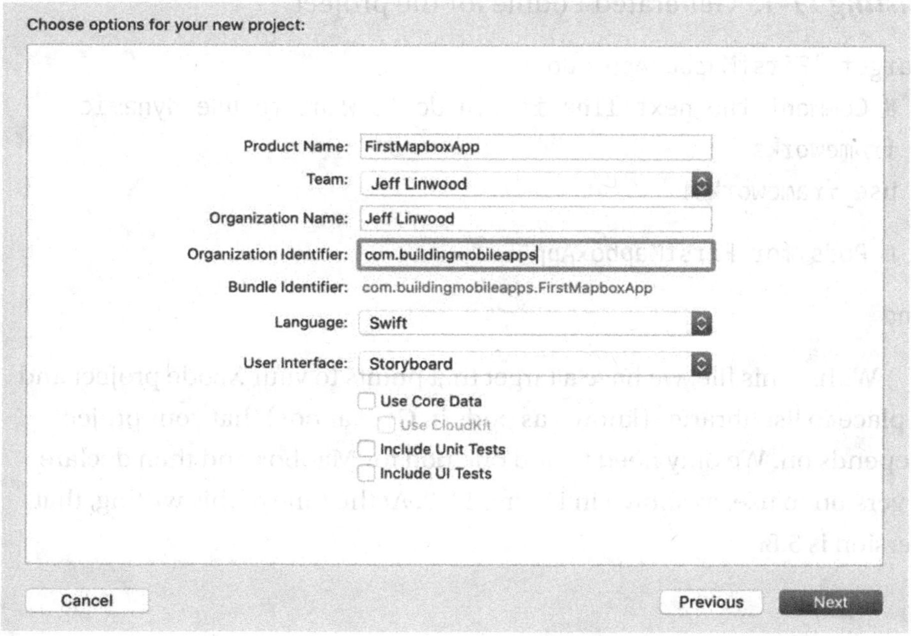

Figure 11-3. *Creating the FirstMapboxApp project in Xcode*

After creating this Xcode project, we need to install the Mapbox SDK. Unlike Google Maps or MapKit, the Mapbox SDK is open source. The easiest way to include the SDK in your application is to use CocoaPods, similar to how we installed the Google Maps for iOS SDK. If you have not installed CocoaPods on your Mac, please visit `https://cocoapods.org/` for installation instructions.

Once you have CocoaPods set up, go to the command line, and change directories into the folder for the project you just created (`FirstMapBoxApp`).

In that directory, create a CocoaPods `Podfile` for your project with this command:

```
pod init
```

The `Podfile` you create will look like Listing 11-1.

Listing 11-1. Generated Podfile for the project

```
target 'FirstMapboxApp' do
  # Comment the next line if you don't want to use dynamic
  frameworks
  use_frameworks!

  # Pods for FirstMapboxApp

end
```

Within this file, we have a target that points to your Xcode project and a place to list libraries (known as pods in CocoaPods) that your project depends on. We only need to add one pod for Mapbox and then declare a version to use, as shown in Listing 11-2. At the time of this writing, that version is 5.8.

Listing 11-2. Added Mapbox CocoaPods library to project

```
target 'FirstMapboxApp' do
  # Comment the next line if you don't want to use dynamic
  frameworks
  use_frameworks!

  # Pods for FirstMapboxApp
  pod 'Mapbox-iOS-SDK', '~> 5.8'
end
```

After editing and saving the Podfile file, run the following command on the command line:

```
pod install
```

CocoaPods will download the Mapbox library and install it into a Pods folder. You will also see a new FirstMapboxApp.xcworkspace file that you will open in Xcode. In this workspace will be your project, plus any dependencies from CocoaPods.

Go ahead and open up the workspace. In your project's Info.plist file (Figure 11-4), add an entry for MGLMapboxAccessToken, and set its string value to be your access token.

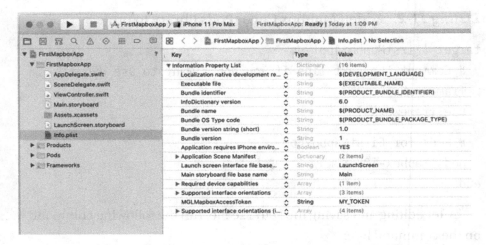

Figure 11-4. *Project Info.plist file with Mapbox access token setting*

Once you have added the access token, we have everything we need to use Mapbox. Let's get started by adding a map to our default view controller.

Displaying a map view

Mapbox provides a map view class named `MGLMapView` (MGL is short for Mapbox GL). To use that map view class in a storyboard, drag a `UIView` onto your view controller, and then change the custom class in the identity inspector to `MGLMapView`, as shown in Figure 11-5.

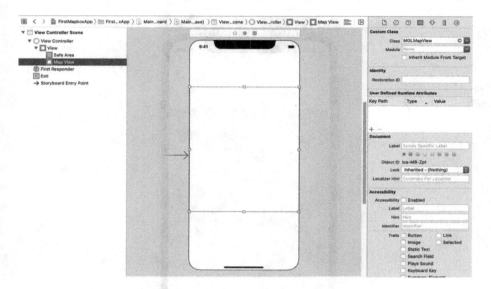

Figure 11-5. *Setting the MGLMapView custom class*

Let's make sure everything is set up. Go ahead and run the application. You should see a basic world map appear in the iOS Simulator, similar to Figure 11-6.

Tip   If you see a blank map with an info button, you may need to double-check your Mapbox access token in the Info.plist file.

Figure 11-6. *Displaying a basic world map in the map view*

Now that we have the map view, let's change the way the map appears by centering it on a new location and choosing a different map style.

Customizing the map view's appearance

Our first task is to create an outlet for our map view, so that we can change its properties programmatically. Use the Xcode Assistant to drag an outlet into the `ViewController` class. Name the outlet `mapView`. The declaration will look like this:

```
@IBOutlet weak var mapView: MGLMapView!
```

You will also need to add an import statement at the top of the class:

```
import Mapbox
```

Now that you have the map view declared as a variable, you can easily center the map over a new location. Inside your `viewDidLoad()` method, add these two lines. Feel free to adjust the latitude and longitude to match your location – the position I picked out is centered over Austin, Texas:

```
mapView.centerCoordinate = CLLocationCoordinate2D(
    latitude: 30.2,
    longitude: -97.75)
mapView.zoomLevel = 10
```

After running the application, you'll see that the map is now showing a lot more detail. Adjusting the zoom level programmatically is easy as well, with a zoom level of 10 being sufficient for central Austin.

One of the best features of Mapbox is the ease of changing how the map renders. You can create your own map styles and then refer to them with a style URL. Or you can use some of the built-in Mapbox styles – these are available through the `MGLStyle` class. Try changing the style URL of your map view to an outdoors style:

```
mapView.styleURL = MGLStyle.outdoorsStyleURL
```

Other map styles available on the `MGLStyle` class are

- `darkStyleURL`
- `lightStyleURL`
- `streetsStyleURL`
- `satelliteStyleURL`
- `ssatelliteStreetsStyleURL`

In Chapter 12, we will examine map styles in much more detail, using the same styleURL property. Let's move on to display a basic marker on the map.

Display a point annotation on the map

The Mapbox SDK supports displaying markers, overlays, and lines on the map as annotations, similar to MapKit or Google Maps for iOS. Let's try a basic example and display a simple map marker, with an associated callout. There are two different steps we need to implement. The first is to create an annotation and display it. The second is to adopt the MGLMapViewDelegate protocol and then implement the mapView: annotationCanShowCallout function. Let's get started by displaying an annotation.

When we work with annotations at a given latitude and longitude, we can use the MGLPointAnnotation class. Instances of this class have properties for their coordinate, title, and subtitle, similar to the MKPointAnnotation class in Apple's MapKit framework. Go ahead and create a function named displayAnnotation, as shown in Listing 11-3. You need to call displayAnnotation() at the end of the viewDidLoad() method.

Listing 11-3. Display an annotation on the map view

```
func displayAnnotation() {
  let annotation = MGLPointAnnotation()
  annotation.coordinate = CLLocationCoordinate2D(
    latitude: 30.25,
    longitude: -97.75)
  annotation.title = "Austin"
  annotation.subtitle = "Texas"
  mapView.addAnnotation(annotation)
}
```

We'll also need to adopt the MGLMapViewDelegate protocol. We can do that with an extension of the ViewController class. Add the extension in Listing 11-4 to the bottom of the ViewController.swift file.

Listing 11-4. Extension for the map view delegate

```
extension ViewController: MGLMapViewDelegate {
  func mapView(_ mapView: MGLMapView,
    annotationCanShowCallout annotation: MGLAnnotation) ->
    Bool {
      return true
  }
}
```

The only method implemented in the delegate controls whether or not a given annotation will show a callout when the user selects it. If we had some annotations that didn't show information, we could have more complicated logic here, but we can just return true. The default behavior for Mapbox will be to show the title and subtitle properties of the annotation in a simple callout.

Last, we need to tell the map view that it has a delegate. Inside the viewDidLoad() method, add this line:

```
mapView.delegate = self
```

We can always implement more methods from the delegate protocol in the future. Go ahead and run the project now, so that you can see how this basic example works. Your code should look similar to Listing 11-5.

Listing 11-5. Complete view controller class for Mapbox

```
import UIKit
import Mapbox

class ViewController: UIViewController {

  @IBOutlet weak var mapView: MGLMapView!

  override func viewDidLoad() {
    super.viewDidLoad()
    // Do any additional setup after loading the view.

    mapView.centerCoordinate =   CLLocationCoordinate2D(
      latitude: 30.2,
      longitude: -97.75)
    mapView.zoomLevel = 10
    mapView.styleURL = MGLStyle.outdoorsStyleURL

    mapView.delegate = self
    displayAnnotation()
  }

  func displayAnnotation() {
    let annotation = MGLPointAnnotation()
    annotation.coordinate = CLLocationCoordinate2D(
      latitude: 30.25,
      longitude: -97.75)
    annotation.title = "Austin"
    annotation.subtitle = "Texas"
    mapView.addAnnotation(annotation)
  }
}
```

```
extension ViewController: MGLMapViewDelegate {
  func mapView(_ mapView: MGLMapView,
    annotationCanShowCallout annotation: MGLAnnotation) ->
    Bool {
      return true
  }
}
```

After running the project in the iOS Simulator and then clicking the marker, you should see something similar to Figure 11-7.

Figure 11-7. *Displaying a marker with a callout on a map view*

This is a straightforward example of how to get started with Mapbox, but we haven't really covered anything that makes Mapbox different from other mapping providers. In the next chapter, we will go in depth on customizing the look and feel of your map with Mapbox. This will give your mobile application a unique personality, and it's pretty easy to do.

CHAPTER 12

Customizing Map Styles with Mapbox

Now that you have seen how to work with the basics of the Mapbox SDK, it's time to look into some of the unique aspects of Mapbox. With Mapbox, you can have almost complete control over the styling and features displayed in your map.

In this chapter, we are going to create a custom map style in Mapbox Studio. We will then use that style with a map in our iOS app.

Most of this chapter will focus on using Mapbox Studio, a web-based tool that lets you customize map styles. The iOS part of this chapter is extremely straightforward, as the Mapbox SDK is easy to work with. We've already seen how to change map styles in the previous chapter, and that is all we will need to do.

Getting ready for map styles

For this project, we will need an iOS application with the Mapbox SDK, a properly configured access token, and a map view on the view controller. You can reuse the project from Chapter 11, or you can create a new application. Your view controller class should have an outlet pointing to the map view on the storyboard named mapView.

© Jeffrey Linwood 2020
J. Linwood, *Build Location Apps on iOS with Swift*,
https://doi.org/10.1007/978-1-4842-6083-8_12

Changing the default style on the map view

As we discussed in the previous chapter, the map view uses a style URL to determine which tiles to load from the server. We discussed the built-in style URLs you can retrieve from the MGLStyle class – dark, light, outdoors, streets, satellite, and satellite with streets. To set these style URLs, you would have code that looked like this:

```
mapView.styleURL = MGLStyle.outdoorsStyleURL
```

Mapbox doesn't limit you to just these built-in styles, however. You can create your own Mapbox styles, which would have a Uniform Resource Indicator (URI) similar to

```
mapbox://styles/jefflinwood/aabb773344
```

The map view object's styleURL property takes URL objects that you can construct yourself with calls to the URL(string:) constructor. Setting the style URL on the map view would look like this:

```
mapView.styleURL = URL(string:mapStyleURI)
```

That is all you need to set up your iOS app to use a custom style that you create. Throughout the remainder of this chapter, we will be working with the web-based Mapbox Studio application to create a custom style. After you save and publish that style, it will have its own mapbox:// URI that you can use with your app.

Creating map styles with Mapbox Studio

Mapbox provides a web-based application, Mapbox Studio, that you can use to customize the maps for your application. These maps can be used in your iOS application, but you can also use them on the Web and in Android applications. All of the styling is done in one place, so that users of your applications have a consistent experience across platforms. Let's start by opening up Mapbox Studio (Figure 12-1) at `https://studio.mapbox.com/`.

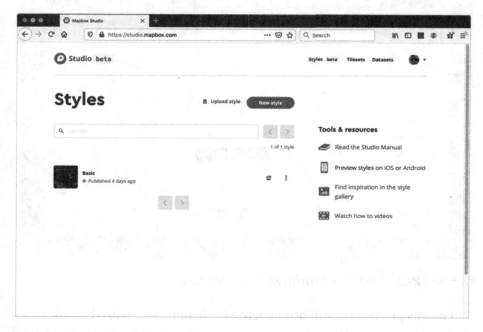

Figure 12-1. *Mapbox Studio*

Browsing through Mapbox Studio, you will find example styles, documentation, and helpful videos. Take a look at some of the tools and resources to see what is new with the application – at the time of writing, Mapbox Studio is in beta release.

Let's go ahead and create a new style. Click the large blue, New Style button on the Studio home screen. You will see a large template selection screen. Take the time to look through all of the different templates and variations (Figure 12-2) – you might find one that really fits your application.

Figure 12-2. *Mapbox Studio style templates*

For this project, we will be using the Basic template, with the Galaxy variation (Figure 12-3) – but you are welcome to create your project with whatever variation you choose.

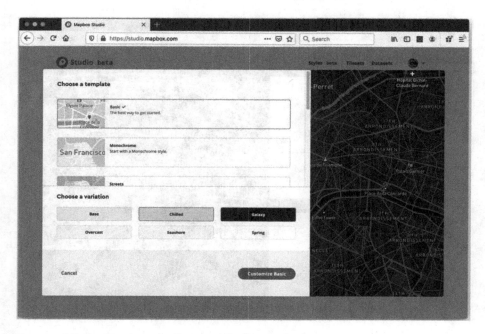

Figure 12-3. *Basic template with the Galaxy variation*

Select Galaxy (or another variation) and then click the Customize Basic button to continue into the detailed style editor, as shown in Figure 12-3.

The style editor (Figure 12-4) has two several different features, but if you would like to customize the display of the map, one of the ways to do this is to adjust the display of the individual layers on the map. The Components view in the left sidebar is the easiest way to do this. For instance, you can select the Road network, choose one of the colors used in the Galaxy variation, and then pick a new color from the color picker. You could similarly update the colors used for water, place labels, or anything else in the map.

Figure 12-4. *Style editor, showing components in left sidebar*

You have full control over which features get displayed on the map, and you can disable them. For instance, if you don't need to show subdivision names on the map, you can easily disable them by selecting the Place labels component in the Components side bar, scrolling down to Settlement subdivisions, and flipping the switch to off, as shown in Figure 12-5.

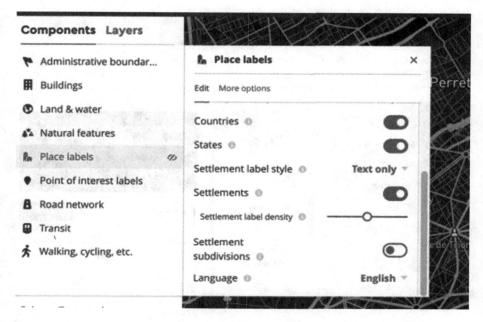

Figure 12-5. *Changing subdivision place name display in Mapbox Studio*

If you are looking for even more fine-grained control, all of the layers are visible under the Layers view in the sidebar, and each layer has a detailed style editor that gives you a very large amount of control.

Choose Layers from the sidebar, pick the state-label layer, and then take a look at the different options. You can choose a different font here, change its size, and adjust text settings (Figure 12-6).

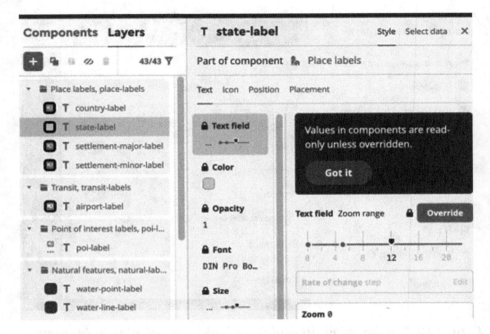

Figure 12-6. *Text styles for place name labels*

We aren't going to change anything at this level for this project, but the option to do it is powerful. Dismiss any open style editors that may be blocking your view of the example map, and then change the viewpoint centered in the map to your location using the search bar with the magnifying glass on the right-hand side of the window (Figure 12-7).

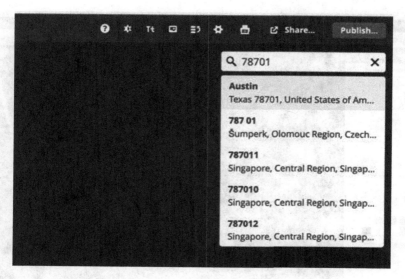

Figure 12-7. *Location picker for Mapbox Studio*

Choose your location, and then zoom in or out until you get the view of the map you would like to see (Figure 12-8).

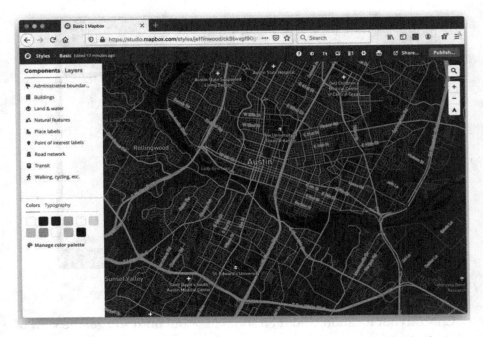

Figure 12-8. *Mapbox Studio showing Austin, Texas, instead of default location*

Explore your area, and if the map style isn't quite what you would like, take some time with the editor to change it!

If you are happy with the map styles or you just want to see this map in your iOS application, click the Publish button at the top right of the editor. A dialog box (Figure 12-9) will appear with your published map style on the left-hand side and the draft version you were editing on the right. This makes it easy to compare and contrast your edits. If everything looks good and you want to replace the existing style, go ahead and click Publish. If you would like to fork your existing style, click Publish as new. If you Publish as new, Mapbox will save your changes as a duplicate, with a name like Basic-copy.

Figure 12-9. *Publish map style dialog box*

After either publishing a new map style or creating a new map style, go back to the Mapbox Studio home screen by clicking the Styles button in the upper left-hand corner. You will see your style listed on the home screen, as in Figure 12-10.

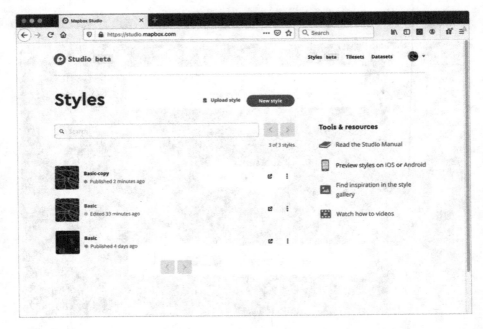

Figure 12-10. *Mapbox Studio home screen with new styles*

Now, let's try our new map style in our iOS app! To the right of your map style, you will see a three-dot button that will open a pop-up menu (Figure 12-11). Click that button, and then click the clipboard icon that appears to copy the Mapbox style URL for your map style.

Figure 12-11. *Pop-up menu for a map style, with Style URL and copy button*

190

Save the style URL, and go back to Xcode. We'll tell the map view to use the style and then run the iOS app with our new map styles.

Displaying the new map style in the app

Copy that style URL into your iOS app, and store it in a constant named mapStyleURI on your ViewController class. Your URL will be unique to your account and style:

```
let mapStyleURI = "mapbox://styles/jefflinwood/zfgwe"
```

Now let's set the map style URL, as we discussed earlier in the chapter:

```
mapView.styleURL = URL(string:mapStyleURI)
```

You can also set the starting location of your map to point to an area you are familiar with. A complete viewDidLoad() method would look like Listing 12-1.

Listing 12-1. The viewDidLoad method, showing the new style URL

```
override func viewDidLoad() {
  super.viewDidLoad()
  // Do any additional setup after loading the view.
  mapView.centerCoordinate = CLLocationCoordinate2D(
            latitude: 30.2,
            longitude: -97.75)
        mapView.zoomLevel = 10
  mapView.styleURL = URL(string: mapStyleURI)
}
```

Be sure to set the mapStyleURI constant in your class. Now run the application, and you will see your new map style, in your iOS application, similar to Figure 12-12.

Figure 12-12. Displaying the new map style in the iOS app

Using Mapbox Studio, you can update the style as you like on the Web, and as long as you publish the changes to the existing style, your iOS app will pick up the changes when it next loads the map.

In the next chapter, we will upload a dataset to Mapbox Studio and then display it in the iOS app. You can use this technique for features you would like to style in Mapbox Studio or if you have too much data to reasonably process as marker annotations on the map because of performance.

CHAPTER 13

Working with Datasets in Mapbox Studio

Using Mapbox Studio, we can add large datasets to our maps as new layers. In this chapter, we will build on top of the custom map style we created in Chapter 12. Once we load in the dataset, we can view it in the map view without changing anything. We'll also see how to retrieve the underlying data features when a user interacts with the map.

This chapter uses the project we created in Chapter 12 with Mapbox Studio as a base. If you have not created the custom map style, and displayed in the map view, go ahead and follow those directions.

Earthquake map

This project involves collecting GeoJSON data about earthquakes, uploading that data as a dataset into Mapbox Studio, and then creating a tileset from the data. When we have a tileset, we can style the appearance of the data in Mapbox Studio, including increasing the size of the data point on the map to match the magnitude of the quake. Then we can display the data in our app and detect when a user taps on one of the earthquakes. When we are done with the project, we should have an app that looks like Figure 13-1.

© Jeffrey Linwood 2020
J. Linwood, *Build Location Apps on iOS with Swift*,
https://doi.org/10.1007/978-1-4842-6083-8_13

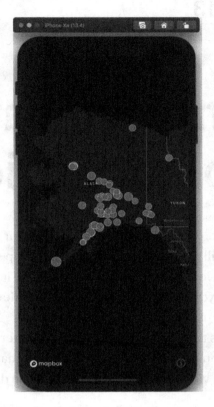

Figure 13-1. *Earthquake data points in the app*

Let's get started with the first step and collect the data we need to show on our map.

Downloading the earthquake data

The earthquakes' dataset we are using for visualization comes from the United States Geological Survey (USGS). If you are curious and want to learn more about earthquake monitoring and research, visit their website at `www.usgs.gov/natural-hazards/earthquake-hazards`.

You can also visit `https://earthquake.usgs.gov/earthquakes/map/` to find a map of earthquakes, refreshed frequently from the server. We will be creating something similar, but with historical earthquake data.

The Earthquake Catalog, which can be accessed at `https://earthquake.usgs.gov/fdsnws/event/1/`, lists all of the different APIs supported by the Earthquake Hazards Program. For our purposes, we are interested in querying historic earthquake information and then returning the results as GeoJSON. GeoJSON is a data encoding format for geographic features, including points, lines, and polygons, along with any associated properties.

The URL we will use to download the data is

```
https://earthquake.usgs.gov/fdsnws/event/1/query?format=geojson
&starttime=2020-01-01&endtime=2020-01-02
```

We specify the start time as January 1, 2020, and the end time as January 2, 2020. We also request GeoJSON back from the server, instead of XML, CSV, or another format. You will see a large GeoJSON file, with 610 different features. Listing 13-1 contains an edited sample of the JSON file, with only one feature and only two of its properties.

Listing 13-1. Sample of GeoJSON response for earthquake API query

```
{
  "type": "FeatureCollection",
  "metadata": {
    "generated": 1587256320000,
    "url": "https://earthquake.usgs.gov/fdsnws/event/1/query?
    format=geojson&starttime=2020-01-01&endtime=2020-01-02",
    "title": "USGS Earthquakes",
    "status": 200,
    "api": "1.8.1",
    "count": 610
  },
```

```
"features": [
  {
    "type": "Feature",
    "properties": {
      "mag": 1.3,
      "title": "M 1.3 - 38km SE of Tanana, Alaska"
    },
    "geometry": {
      "type": "Point",
      "coordinates": [
        -151.59520000000001,
        64.892200000000003,
        2.5
      ]
    },
    "id": "ak02021ksej"
  }
],
"bbox": [
  -179.2752,
  -53.0907,
  -1.75,
  175.8577,
  69.6006,
  392.48
]
}
```

Make the API call, and then download the results to a GeoJSON file –
try using a web browser or the `curl` command. The GeoJSON file is also
included in the downloadable source code for the book, in Chapter 13
folder. Feel free to try other date ranges with the API, if you like. For this
particular project, we will be using the `mag` property (the magnitude of the
earthquake), so other GeoJSON sources may not be an exact match for the
process. The concepts used here would translate well to other projects,
however.

We will take the list of earthquakes that we just downloaded and then
upload them to Mapbox Studio next.

Creating a dataset on Mapbox Studio

Mapbox Studio lets you save and edit collections of GeoJSON features in
the cloud, such as the earthquake data we just downloaded. These datasets
can be turned into tilesets, which then may be edited in the Mapbox Studio
style editor we used in Chapter 12. We will go through this entire process,
from uploading a dataset to styling the features in the editor.

Let's start by creating a dataset on Mapbox Studio. Visit the Datasets
page (Figure 13-2) on Mapbox Studio (`https://studio.mapbox.com/
datasets/`), or click the Datasets link in the upper right-hand corner. You
will see any datasets you have already created or the option to upload a
new dataset.

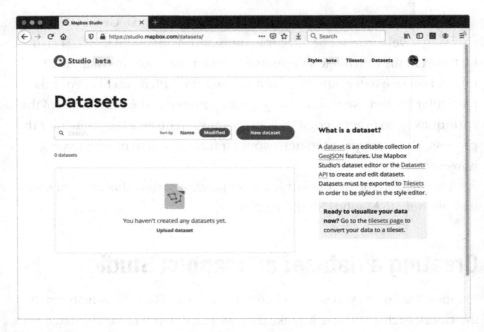

Figure 13-2. *Mapbox Studio Datasets web page*

Clicking the large blue New dataset button will pop up a dialog box offering the option of either creating a blank dataset or uploading a GeoJSON file. Choose Upload in the tab bar of the dialog box (Figure 13-3).

Figure 13-3. *Upload a new dataset to Mapbox Studio*

Select the GeoJSON file you downloaded in the previous section of this chapter, and then upload it. Mapbox Studio will process the file and find all of the GeoJSON features (Figure 13-4).

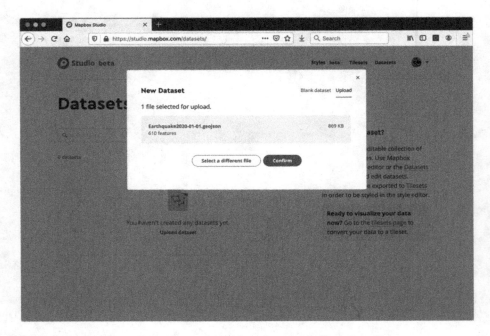

Figure 13-4. *Confirm dataset upload to Mapbox Studio*

If the number of features Mapbox found matches the number of features you would expect to see in your GeoJSON file, click the Confirm button. You may name your dataset to be whatever you like, but the default will be the name of the file you uploaded. In our case, that would be Earthquake2020-01-01. If that name works, click the Create button.

Mapbox Studio will import the features, and you will see a confirmation message, similar to the following dialog box in Figure 13-5.

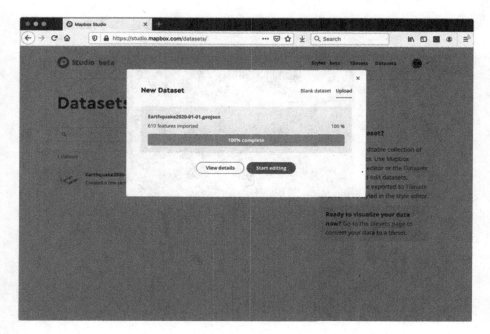

Figure 13-5. *Dataset upload confirmation dialog box*

If you start editing the dataset, you will see the dataset plotted against a simple map background (Figure 13-6). You can select any of the points in the dataset and either inspect or modify the data.

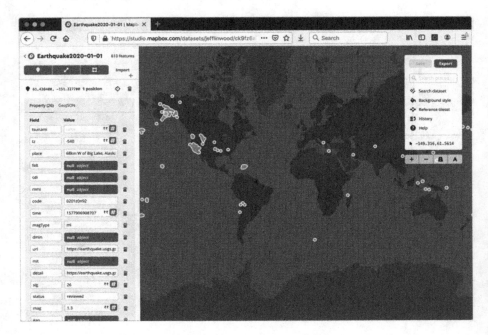

Figure 13-6. *Dataset editor showing an earthquake point*

In our case, we are using clean data from the API, so we do not need to inspect the data for anomalies or to clear up missing values. We can also take a quick glance at the data and see if the dataset we just imported makes sense and matches where we would expect to see data points.

This dataset imported correctly, and we can create a tileset from this dataset. The difference between a dataset and a tileset is that we will be able to modify how the data appears in the map in a tileset, instead of editing the data values in the the dataset.

Click the blue Mapbox icon in the upper left-hand corner to go back to the Datasets screen (Figure 13-7) or navigate to `https://studio.mapbox.com/datasets/` in your web browser. Select the three-dot pop-up menu next to the earthquake dataset you just uploaded, and then choose View details from the pop-up menu.

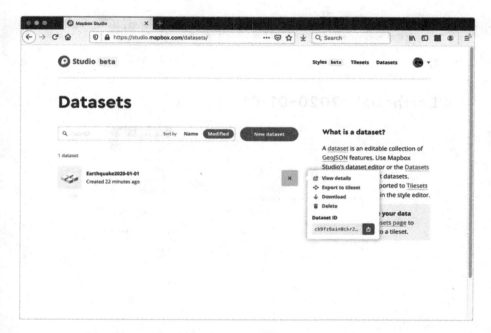

Figure 13-7. *Pop-up menu to view details for a dataset*

The dataset details screen that appears in Figure 13-8 allows you to export this dataset to a tileset.

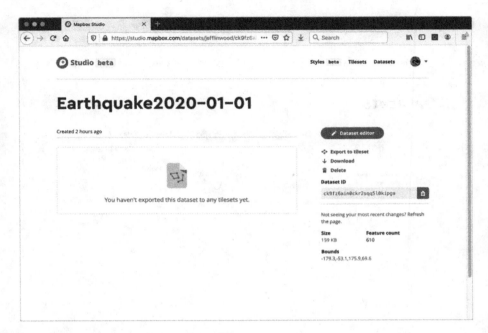

Figure 13-8. *Dataset details screen*

In the next section, we will create a tileset. This tileset is what we use in the Mapbox Studio style editor to change the appearance of the data in the map.

Creating a tileset

From the details screen of a dataset, Mapbox Studio provides an easy way to create a tileset. Click the Export to tileset link in the right-hand column. A dialog box (Figure 13-9) appears asking if you want to export to a new tileset or to update a connected tileset.

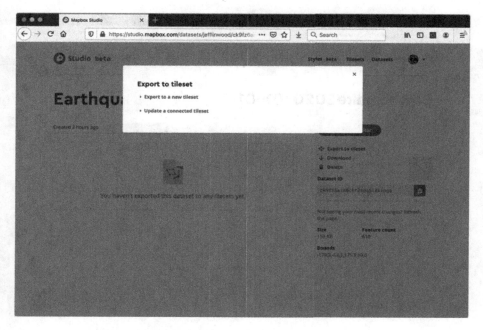

Figure 13-9. *Export to tileset dialog box*

We will export to a new tileset, so click that link. A text box will appear
with a suggested name for the tileset (the same as the dataset). If that
works, click Export, and then Mapbox will process the dataset into a tileset.
After this conversion is complete, you will see that a connected tileset
appears on the dataset details screen (Figure 13-10).

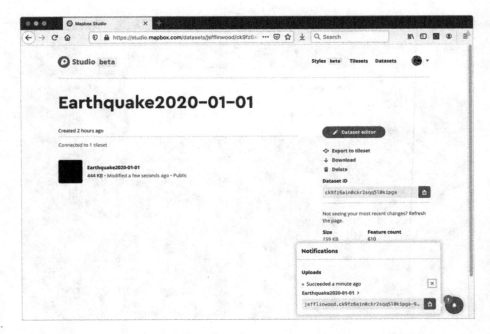

Figure 13-10. *Connected tileset along with processing notification on dataset details screen*

If you click the tileset, you will get a preview of the data in the tileset, as it would be laid out on a map. This can be useful to make sure the dataset export processed correctly.

Our next step will be to add this tileset to the map style we created in Chapter 12. If you have not created a map style yet, go ahead and follow the directions in Chapter 12.

Adding the tileset to a style

We now need to open up our map style to add the tileset as a layer. Click the Styles tab in the upper right-hand corner of the web page or navigate to https://studio.mapbox.com/ to see the list of your styles. Choose the map style you created in the last chapter, and click it to enter the style editor.

In the style editor, choose the Layers tab in the left-hand sidebar. We need to add a new layer, so click the plus button in the upper right-hand side of the Layers tab. When the New layer window appears, a list of data sources will appear, including historical election results.

Type earthquake into the filter box, and you will see your tileset appear (Figure 13-11).

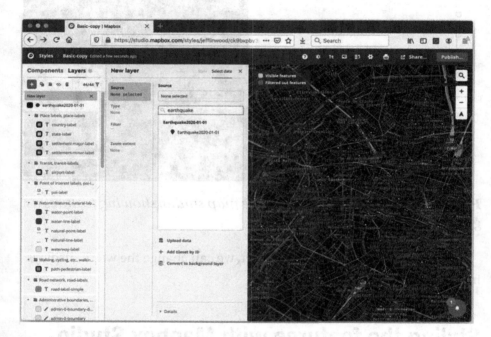

Figure 13-11. *Adding a tileset to the map style*

Select the tileset in the search results window, and then zoom to a different part of the world that is tectonically active and has earthquakes, like Alaska. You will see the features from the GeoJSON we uploaded on your map, as in Figure 13-12. The green dots are for reference and are not how the tileset will initially display. They show that all of your data is going to display in the map – you can apply a filter that will not show certain data based on conditions. If a data point is filtered out, that data will appear as a red dot here.

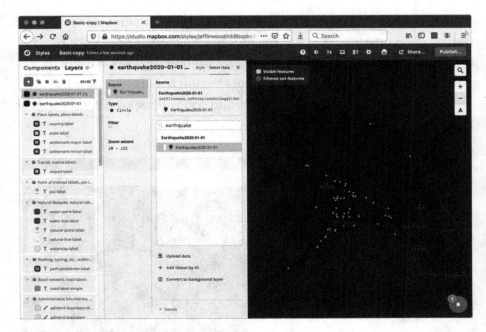

Figure 13-12. *Added a tileset to the map studio, showing features as green dots*

Now that we have added the tileset, we can change the way it displays in any map that uses this style.

Styling the features with Mapbox Studio

On the layers sidebar, find the earthquake tileset you just added. Click it, and you will see a layer style editing palette appear as a window (Figure 13-13).

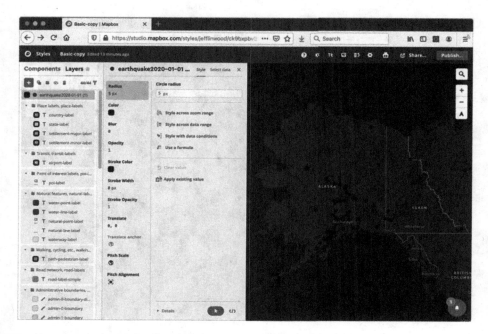

Figure 13-13. *Default tiles for the earthquake layer*

It may be hard to see, but each data point on the map is being shown as a 5 pixel circle, with a black fill, and no outline. This doesn't provide very good contrast on a dark map, so let's change the fill color (the property marked color). Select that color property, and a color picker appears. Choose a brighter color, such as red. You will immediately see your data points change color on the map, as in Figure 13-14, if you are looking at an area that had earthquakes.

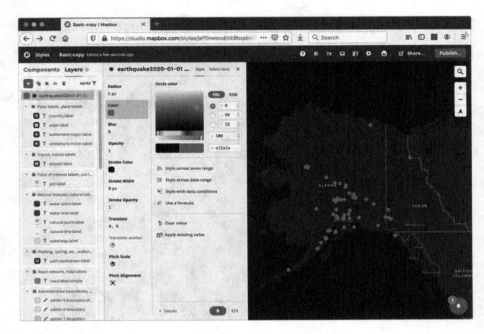

Figure 13-14. *Data points with a red fill color*

You can also change the stroke color and the stroke outline to give the data points even more contrast. Try setting the stroke color to the hexadecimal color value ece9e9 and adjusting the stroke width to 1 pixel. You can also choose your own colors here too, if you like; it won't affect the project.

Next, let's try and convey some information about the magnitude of the earthquake with the radius of the circle we use to display the point. Mapbox Studio lets you vary properties of the map style with the properties for each feature of the map. Select the radius, and then select the link that says Style across data range. You will see a data field chooser pop up that lets you find a numeric data field. Look for the mag data field, which is short for magnitude (Figure 13-15).

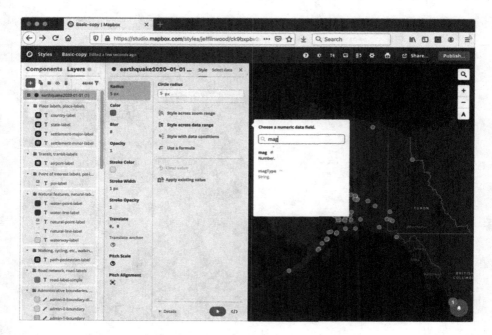

Figure 13-15. *Choosing the magnitude data field to vary the radius field*

After choosing the magnitude field, you will have several options appear to vary the radius. We are going to do a simple linear interpolation between the lowest magnitude, with 5 pixels, and the largest magnitude with 15 pixels.

Figure 13-16 shows the radius setting for the circle, after choosing to style across the data range with the magnitude field.

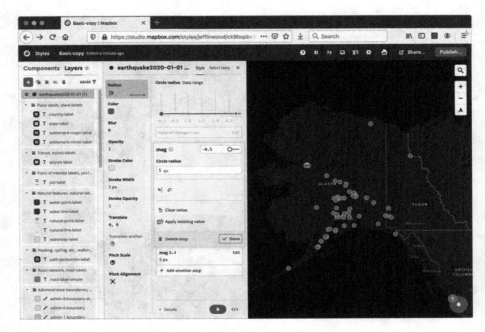

Figure 13-16. *Editing the radius data settings for the earthquake data*

This settings view can be somewhat confusing. There are two stops for a linear interpolation of the magnitude data point – the lowest value, at –0.5, and the highest value, at 5.4. Both have a circle radius of 5 pixels, so there is no variation.

What we want to do is to leave the lowest setting alone and change the highest value. Click the bottom value, 5.4, and then change the circle radius to 15 px, as in Figure 13-17. You will see the line chart immediately start to show the radius value rising from left to right. Do not modify the value with the slider that you see – unless you want to change one of the stop values.

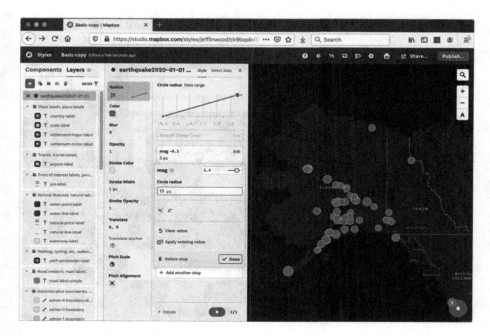

Figure 13-17. *Adjusting the radius to vary with the magnitude linearly*

Be sure to click Done to save the changes to the radius. You could add more stops here, in case you want to set the radius for an intermediate value.

You could also change the other values, such as color or stroke size to vary with magnitude, or one of the other properties in your dataset. Feel free to experiment with this.

Now, let's publish our map style changes. Click the large blue Publish button in the upper right-hand side of the screen, as shown in Figure 13-17. After clicking Publish, a dialog box will appear to let you confirm your changes with a visual display of the differences (Figure 13-18).

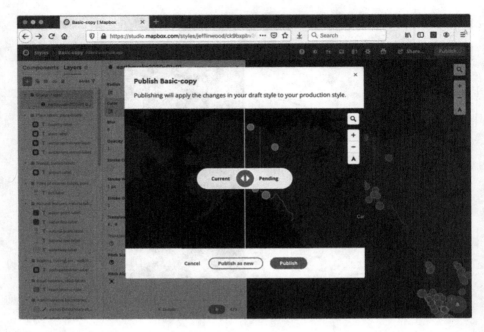

Figure 13-18. *Publishing changes to the map style*

You can see your data additions in this dialog box, with the new map styles you applied. If everything looks good, click Publish, and your changes will be live for any websites or mobile apps that use this map style. If you would like to publish a new version of this map style, for instance, to avoid changing the look and feel for existing users, you can do that as well through this dialog box.

You will get a nice confirmation message about your style being successfully published (Figure 13-19).

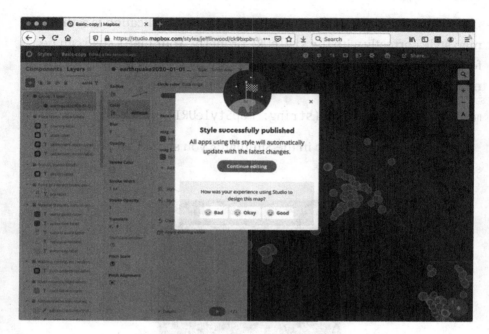

Figure 13-19. *Publish confirmation message for map styles*

We can now leave Mapbox Studio and open up Xcode to see our changes in the app.

Displaying the dataset in the app

Running the app from Chapter 12 should display the map style you just edited, with the earthquake data points. No code changes should be needed. If you do not see the earthquake data, make sure you published the map styles in Mapbox Studio, and you are viewing a part of the world that has earthquakes.

The following code snippet will show much of the state of Alaska in your map:

```
mapView.centerCoordinate = CLLocationCoordinate2D(
          latitude: 61.2,
          longitude: -149.9)
mapView.zoomLevel = 3
```

You may also want to double-check that your application is setting the map style correctly with the `styleURL` property. Your map's style can be found from the Mapbox Studio home screen by clicking the pop-up menu next to the style and copying the style URL found there:

```
mapView.styleURL = URL(string: mapStyleURI)
```

After running your app in the Simulator, you should see something similar to Figure 13-20.

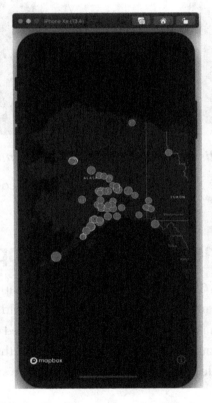

Figure 13-20. *Earthquake data points in the app*

While these data points are not map markers like we used in Chapter 11, they are features we can detect when a user taps on the map. For the final part of this project, let's print some information on the console when a user taps on a data point.

Detecting a tap on the features

To do something when a user taps on the map, we need to add a standard UIKit tap gesture recognizer to the map view. The MGLMapView class already has several tap recognizers that it uses to detect user input for map operations like scrolling and zooming. We need to add a tap gesture recognizer, and only have it do something if the built-in tap gesture recognizers do not handle the tap. This is a common pattern for Mapbox map views and not limited to the use case of detecting taps for data features.

Add the method in Listing 13-2 to your ViewController class, and then call the addGestureRecognizer() function from the view controller's viewDidLoad() method.

Listing 13-2. Adding a tap gesture recognizer to the map view

```
func addGestureRecognizer() {
  let tapGR = UITapGestureRecognizer(target: self,
      action: #selector(mapTapped(sender:)))

  for recognizer in mapView.gestureRecognizers!
      where recognizer is UITapGestureRecognizer {
      tapGR.require(toFail: recognizer)
  }
  mapView.addGestureRecognizer(tapGR)
}
```

The tap gesture recognizer will call a method named
mapTapped(sender:)) that we also need to implement. When the map is
tapped, we will ask the map view to identify any features at that point, and
then we will list them to the console. You can also ask the map view to only
show you features in a certain layer or layers, if you want.

The mapTapped(sender:)) method will need an @objc annotation
for the selector to work. The implementation of this method will look like
Listing 13-3.

Listing 13-3. Looking up visible map features when a user taps the
app

```
@objc func mapTapped(sender: UITapGestureRecognizer) {
  let mapPoint = sender.location(in: mapView)

  let features = mapView.visibleFeatures(at: mapPoint)
  print(features)
}
```

Add the preceding method to the app, and then run the app. Be sure
to add a call to addGestureRecognizer() in your viewDidLoad() method
as well. When you tap on one of the earthquake circles, you will see the
properties of the feature output on the console in Xcode.

Conclusion

This is the simplest possible implementation here – we could easily extend
this out to update labels in an in-app UI (such as a bottom toolbar) with
information about the data point, for instance. The earthquake data
features returned by the map would be MGLPointFeature objects. If we
had uploaded GeoJSON data with polylines or polygons, those would
have been other classes that implement the MGLFeature protocol, such as
MGLPolylineFeature or MGLPolygonFeature.

This was a fairly involved project, but I hope you enjoyed working with some real data and building out a visualization using the Mapbox Studio.

In our next chapter, we step away from Mapbox Studio and turn our attention to providing driving directions with Mapbox. We will create an app that provides a turn-by-turn directions user experience with the Mapbox Navigation framework.

CHAPTER 14

Turn-by-Turn Navigation with Mapbox

In addition to the Mapbox mapping SDK for iOS, Mapbox offers a turn-by-turn navigation user interface SDK for iOS as well. Typically, this style of navigation would be used for an app that provides built-in driving directions, such as a rideshare service or a package delivery service.

We will build a simple navigation app in this chapter that routes from the user's current location to a destination. We will use the standard turn-by-turn user interface that Mapbox provides, known as the Mapbox Navigation framework. If you would like to build your own user interface, you can use the Mapbox Core Navigation framework to power that user interface with route updates. The Mapbox Navigation framework is built on top of the Mapbox Core Navigation framework.

In either case, your application uses the Mapbox Directions API to create routes between origins and destinations. As with other Mapbox APIs, check the pricing for the Directions API before building it into your application, to make sure that you understand how the free tier and tiered pricing works.

© Jeffrey Linwood 2020
J. Linwood, *Build Location Apps on iOS with Swift*,
https://doi.org/10.1007/978-1-4842-6083-8_14

Setting up your app project

Before we can dive into the Mapbox Navigation framework, we will need to create a new iOS application project, set it up with CocoaPods, and then add some capabilities and Info.plist entries.

Start by creating a new iOS Single View Application in Xcode. Name the app MapboxNavigationApp. Choose the same defaults as we have used in previous projects, to use storyboard/UIKit and Swift.

Setting up CocoaPods

Once you generate the iOS application, close the project in Xcode, and open the command line in the same directory as the project. We will initialize CocoaPods for this project and then edit the Podfile to include the Mapbox Navigation framework. Generate a Podfile with the following command:

```
pod init
```

Once you create a Podfile, open it up in a text editor, and include the Mapbox Navigation framework as a dependency. Your complete Podfile should look like Listing 14-1.

Listing 14-1. Podfile for app that uses the Mapbox Navigation framework

```
target 'MapboxNavigationApp' do
  # Comment the next line if you don't want to use dynamic
  frameworks
  use_frameworks!

  # Pods for MapboxNavigationApp
  pod 'MapboxNavigation', '~> 0.39.0'
end
```

Close the text editor and save the Podfile. Then from the command line, install the dependencies with the following command:

```
pod install
```

After you install the CocoaPods, you need to open the MapboxNavigationApp.xcworkspace workspace in Xcode, not the Xcode project.

Adding entries to Info.plist

The next step that we need to do to use the Mapbox SDK is to add two entries to the Info.plist file in your Xcode workspace. Open up that file, and add these two properties:

- MGLMapboxAccessToken

- Privacy - Location When In Use Usage Description

The access token entry can be the same access token you have already used in previous Mapbox chapters (see Chapter 11 for instructions). The location usage description will appear to the user the first time the app accesses their location. A sample description might be "This app will use your location to provide in-app navigation and to improve the map".

This takes care of the Info.plist file settings. We also need to add capabilities to the application so that the app works in background mode.

Adding required capabilities

The Mapbox Navigation framework requires two different background mode capabilities. If you don't set the background audio mode, the app will crash immediately and tell you to add it. While you can add these background modes through the Info.plist file, you can also add them as capabilities through the Xcode project.

Select the MapboxNavigationApp target in Xcode, and then select the **Signing & Capabilities** tab. Click the **+ Capability** button to add a capability. Choose **Background Modes** from the list of capabilities, as shown in Figure 14-1.

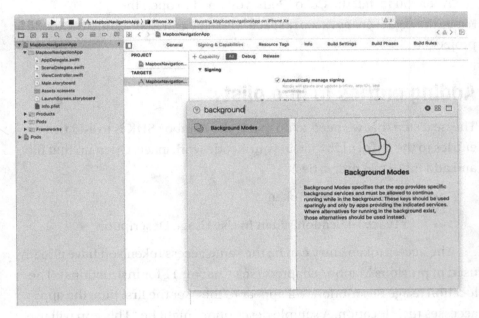

Figure 14-1. *Adding background mode capability to app target*

Select **Audio, Airplay, and Picture in Picture**, as well as **Location updates** (Figure 14-2).

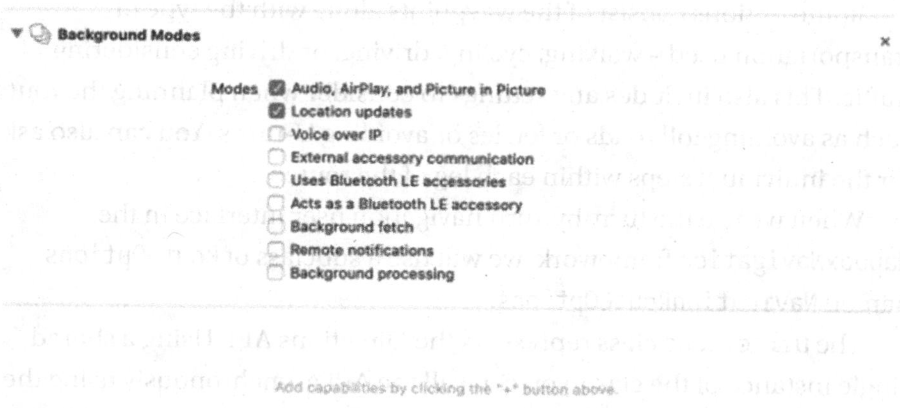

▼ 🔄 Background Modes   ×

Modes ☑ Audio, AirPlay, and Picture in Picture
       ☑ Location updates
       ☐ Voice over IP
       ☐ External accessory communication
       ☐ Uses Bluetooth LE accessories
       ☐ Acts as a Bluetooth LE accessory
       ☐ Background fetch
       ☐ Remote notifications
       ☐ Background processing

Add capabilities by clicking the "+" button above.

Figure 14-2. *Selecting background modes for navigation*

Now we have everything set up to use the Mapbox Navigation framework. Let's move on to the Mapbox Directions API.

Using the Mapbox Directions API

Your app needs to calculate a route between two or more different waypoints, using the Mapbox Directions API. While you can make HTTPS calls to the Directions API directly, it's much easier to use the helper classes in the `MapboxDirections` framework.

The key classes that you need to get started with the Mapbox Directions API are `Waypoint`, `RouteOptions`, `Directions`, and `Route`.

Waypoints are the places on the route. You can have up to 25 waypoints for directions when cycling or walking. You may also have up to 25 waypoints if you are driving, but don't want the route to consider traffic. If you do want to consider traffic conditions, you can only have two or three waypoints.

Route options consist of the waypoints along with the type of transportation used – walking, cycling, driving, or driving considering traffic. This also includes any settings to consider when planning the route, such as avoiding toll roads or ferries or avoiding U-turns. You can also ask for the individual steps within each leg of the route.

When we use the turn-by-turn navigation user interface in the `MapboxNavigation` framework, we will use a subclass of `RouteOptions` named `NavigationRouteOptions`.

The `Directions` class represents the Directions API. Using a shared single instance of the class, you can call the API asynchronously using the `calculate(_:completionHandler:)` method. Pass the route options as the first argument and a closure as the second argument.

Last, a successful directions call will pass at least one route as argument to the completion handler. A route will have one leg (a `RouteLeg` object) if it has two waypoints and one leg for every additional waypoint.

Putting all of this together, we can write two simple methods that will create the waypoints for our directions request and then make the call to the directions API.

The first method (Listing 14-2) creates the waypoints, in this case a trip between Austin, Texas, and the Alamo in San Antonio, Texas. You could use the user's current location as the first waypoint if you wanted.

Listing 14-2. Create waypoints for Mapbox directions

```
func createWaypoints() -> [Waypoint] {
  let austinCoordinate = CLLocationCoordinate2D(
              latitude: 30.27, longitude: -97.74)
  let alamoCoordinate = CLLocationCoordinate2D(
        latitude: 29.426, longitude: -98.486)

  let austin = Waypoint(coordinate: austinCoordinate,
                        name: "Austin")
```

```
    let alamo = Waypoint(coordinate: alamoCoordinate,
                         name: "The Alamo")
    return [austin, alamo]
}
```

Add that `createWaypoints()` method to your `ViewController` class. You can also see that constructing a waypoint is fairly straightforward.

The `getDirections()` method in Listing 14-3 passes those waypoints into a new `RouteOptions` instance and then calls the Mapbox Directions API. This will fail if you have not set the Mapbox access token properly in your project. We then iterate through each step in the only leg of the route. If we had more than two waypoints, we would have additional legs. There are many different properties on the route, leg, and step objects such as estimated time, distance in meters, and headings (for steps) that you can inspect on your own – some may be useful for a custom user interface, and others may be unnecessary.

Listing 14-3. Getting directions from the Mapbox Directions API

```
func getDirections() {
  let waypoints = createWaypoints()
  let options = RouteOptions(waypoints: waypoints,
                  profileIdentifier: .automobile)
  options.includesSteps = true

  Directions.shared.calculate(options) {
    (waypoints, routes, error) in
    guard let route = routes?.first else {
        print(error ?? "No Error")
        return
    }
    guard let firstLeg = route.legs.first else {
        return
    }
```

```
    print(firstLeg.name)
    for step in firstLeg.steps {
        print(step.instructions)
    }
  }
}
```

Try this function out by calling getDirections() from your viewDidLoad() method and then looking for output in the console.

You could build on top of the preceding function yourself to add the coordinates from the route onto your Mapbox map as a polyline. Instead, we are going to use the much simpler approach of using the prebuilt turn-by-turn navigation user interface in the MapboxNavigation framework.

Displaying the navigation user interface

To display the default navigation user interface, we need to create a NavigationViewController and then present it modally from our ViewController class. We can either do this completely programmatically or add a storyboard reference for the navigation view controller and then configure it in the prepareForSegue method of our view controller. We won't use the storyboard on this project. Also, just for clarity, this is a different class and serves a different purpose than the UINavigationController class from Apple's UIKit framework.

We are going to build on the code we discussed earlier, but make a few changes. For instance, we can keep the way that we create waypoints, but we are going to use the NavigationRouteOptions class instead of RouteOptions – the navigation route options comes with configuration optimized for turn-by-turn navigation. Instead of printing out some of the route properties, we are going to create an instance of the NavigationViewController class with the route as an argument. After we create that instance, we present it modally as a full-screen view controller. There is a built-in dismiss button at the bottom of the navigation view controller that would return the user to our original view controller.

We also take the opportunity to add a feature to our route request, which is to avoid toll roads. You can also choose to avoid ferries, motorways, restricted roads, or tunnels. All of these are enumerated on the MBRoadClasses class. Only one of these may be avoided, not a combination, even though the API allows for an array of road classes.

Listing 14-4 is our startNavigation() method. You can see how it mostly differs from the existing getDirections() method in the closure.

Listing 14-4. Start navigation with turn-by-turn directions in a user interface

```
func startNavigation() {
  let waypoints = createWaypoints()
  let options = NavigationRouteOptions(
                waypoints:waypoints)
  options.roadClassesToAvoid = [.toll]

  Directions.shared.calculate(options) {
    (waypoints, routes, error) in
    guard let route = routes?.first else {
        print(error ?? "No error")
        return
    }
    let navVC = NavigationViewController(for: route)
    navVC.modalPresentationStyle = .fullScreen
    self.present(navVC,
                animated: true,
                completion: nil)
  }
}
```

Call the `startNavigation()` method from your `viewDidLoad()` method. You can replace the `getDirections()` method we created in Chapter 13. You will see a map view with instructions, an estimated time of arrival, and the remaining distance, similar to Figure 14-3.

Figure 14-3. *Turn-by-turn navigation in the app*

Now that you have the user interface up and running, explore how it works – you can swipe left and right at the top to navigate between different steps in the route. Press the x button in the lower right to dismiss the navigation view controller when you are finished.

Using the Mapbox simulated navigation

While you can certainly use a GPX file to simulate navigation with the iOS Simulator, you may want to use the simulation that Mapbox provides for a route. This is useful for testing, as it sticks to the route you asked for, and lets you change the speed, as you can see in Figure 14-4.

Figure 14-4. *Simulating navigation, sped up to nine times normal speed*

To use simulation with Mapbox, you will need to modify the startNavigation() method. Rather than creating the NavigationViewController with just the route, you will need to create a navigation service, use that to populate navigation options, and then pass that to the NavigationViewController.

The navigation service (MapboxNavigationService) gets instantiated with the route and the .always enum for the simulating argument:

```
let navService = MapboxNavigationService(
    route: route, simulating: .always)
```

Use that navigation service to create an instance of NavigationOptions:

```
let navOptions = NavigationOptions(
  navigationService: navService)
```

We will pass those options to the navigation view controller, along with the route. The route itself does not change when you use navigation simulation:

```
let navVC = NavigationViewController(for: route,
                              options: navOptions)
```

Putting the preceding lines of code into our startNavigation() method and replacing the call to create the Mapbox navigation view controller, our final method looks like Listing 14-5.

Listing 14-5. Starting navigation with a simulated drive

```
func startNavigation() {
  let waypoints = createWaypoints()
  let options = NavigationRouteOptions(
      waypoints:waypoints)
  options.roadClassesToAvoid = [.toll]
```

```
Directions.shared.calculate(options) {
  (waypoints, routes, error) in
  guard let route = routes?.first else {
    print(error ?? "No error")
    return
  }
  let navService = MapboxNavigationService(
    route: route, simulating: .always)
  let navOptions = NavigationOptions(
    navigationService: navService)
  let navVC = NavigationViewController(for: route,
                                    options: navOptions)
  navVC.modalPresentationStyle = .fullScreen
  self.present(navVC,
              animated: true,
              completion: nil)
  }
}
```

After you replace your startNavigation() method with the Swift code in Listing 14-5, run your project. You should expect to see a sped-up drive through the route between your start and finish.

Customizing the navigation experience

If you don't like the display of the app, you can create custom styles for the user interface, including day and night variants. These styles can use your Mapbox map styles for tiles, and they can also use the UIAppearance protocol to style individual user interface elements. For instance, you could use this to match the colors you use for your brand, so the navigation looks like it belongs with the app.

There are many other features built into the Navigation SDK as well, such as CarPlay support, spoken voice options, and determining which side of the road to use for a waypoint (useful for rideshare or delivery apps).

If you like, you can create your own navigation user interface using the `MapboxCoreNavigation` framework. You would need to listen for `routeControllerProgressDidChange` notifications. These notifications contain location updates in the form of a `RouteProgress` class that you would use to update your user interface. You can get information about the distance traveled, distance remaining, remaining legs and steps, and other information. You can also get more granular information about progress in the current leg and the current step. The current step progress provides information about the next intersection, the distance to the next intersection, the distance until the next maneuver a user makes, and other information you could use for a user interface.

Conclusion

If the turn-by-turn navigation user experience helps your application, using Mapbox's prebuilt components makes this very easy. Compared to building your own solution on top of another directions API, you can have a simpler experience for the user and less code to maintain within your application.

In Chapter 15, we look at Mapbox's offline map capabilities – this is one of the areas where Mapbox provides a technology solution that other mapping SDKs don't replicate.

CHAPTER 15

Using Offline Maps with Mapbox

Many mobile applications need to work in areas with no or limited cellular coverage. If you as a developer want to provide mapping functionality, there are a few ways to do this, but the best way would be to use a map framework that you can use either online or offline. The Mapbox SDK for iOS provides the capability to download offline map tiles and then store them on the user's phone for use in a map view later. I've used this offline functionality to create a hiking app for the New Mexico mountains and to provide maps for kids with iPads on road trips.

We will use the offline pack technology with Mapbox maps to download a region of the map for offline use in this chapter. Then you can try setting your phone to airplane mode to see how the app works with the offline tiles.

As with other mapping APIs, check the pricing for offline map tiles, and make sure that it matches your use case.

Setting up your app project

This project builds on the basics of Mapbox in Chapter 11, including setting up a project and obtaining an access token. Create a new project in Xcode, named OfflineMapsApp. You can also reuse the FirstMapboxApp project from Chapter 11, if you like.

© Jeffrey Linwood 2020
J. Linwood, *Build Location Apps on iOS with Swift*,
https://doi.org/10.1007/978-1-4842-6083-8_15

The project will be a Single View Application with Swift and storyboard, similar to all of our previous projects.

Run `pod init` in your project's directory to generate the `Podfile`. Add the Mapbox SDK to your CocoaPods file, as seen in Listing 15-1.

Listing 15-1. Podfile for the offline maps app

```
target 'OfflineMapsApp' do
  use_frameworks!

  # Pods for OfflineMapsApp
  pod 'Mapbox-iOS-SDK', '~> 5.8'
end
```

Now run `pod install` to set up the Mapbox SDK with your project. Open the workspace file with Xcode from now on, instead of the project file.

Add your Mapbox access token to the `Info.plist` file as the `MGLMapboxAccessToken` entry. Also add a Mapbox map view to the view controller. Create an outlet variable in the view controller, named `mapView`. You should also import the `Mapbox` framework at the top of the view controller class.

All of this is covered in more detail in Chapter 11, so if you want to see more specific instructions for any of these steps, follow that chapter first.

Understanding offline map downloading

Most map engines, whether on Web or mobile, will cache downloaded map tiles to provide better performance or to reduce bandwidth costs. For instance, with the Mapbox SDK for iOS, that cache will contain up to 50 megabytes of tiles or style information. Mapbox goes one step beyond this and lets you as a developer create an offline pack of map tiles, represented by the `MGLOfflinePack` class. Your app downloads map tiles from Mapbox based on the geographic coordinates and zoom level you choose. This combination is known as the region and can be used with the protocol MGLOfflineRegion. The only implementation of this protocol is in the MGLTilePyramidOfflineRegion class.

While the map tiles download, your app can process status updates, so you know what the progress of the download is and when it is complete. Mapbox will fire off several notifications to observe. The offline pack is the userInfo variable on the notification. Each offline pack has an associated progress variable, which contains an MGLOfflinePackProgress structure. On this structure, you can get the number of resources downloaded, bytes downloaded, tiles downloaded, and a minimum and maximum number of resources left to download. This way, you can provide the user with a progress bar, a spinner with a progress message, or something else to inform them of the download.

Estimating the number of tiles used

When creating your application, be very mindful of the maximum number of tiles you will let a user download, especially if you create a mass-market application and provide the application for free. Mapbox will allow you to download up to 6000 map tiles per user as its default, but you can override that setting and download more.

If you don't have a good idea about how many tiles to provide for your users, try the Mapbox offline tile count estimator tool (Figure 15-1) at https://docs.mapbox.com/playground/offline-estimator/.

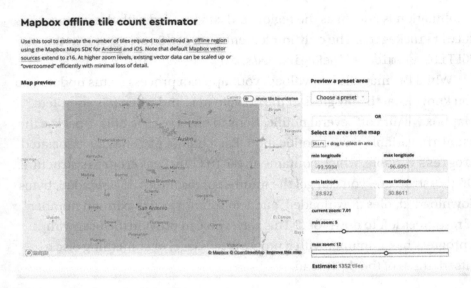

Figure 15-1. *Mapbox offline tile count estimator*

Because Mapbox uses vector tiles, you can have your apps zoom to levels below the max zoom setting that you download, for instance, you could download offline map tiles for this region of Central Texas, from a minimum zoom of 5 to a maximum zoom of 12.

Your map could still zoom in further to zoom level 13 or 14; it would just be missing any additional details at those levels. The maximum zoom level for Mapbox vector tiles is 16, so you can't request tiles beyond that level.

Downloading an offline map pack

The first step to download an offline map pack is to define the geographic bounds for the area. This could be a defined area, with northeast and southwest corners, or you could just use the bounds of the map currently displayed in the map view.

To create your own bounds, create a function in your `ViewController` class from the code in Listing 15-2 – these coordinates define an area in Central Texas, the same ones we used for the offline map tile estimator.

Listing 15-2. Creating offline region bounds

```
func createOfflineRegionBounds() -> MGLCoordinateBounds {
  let southwest = CLLocationCoordinate2D(
      latitude: 28.822,
      longitude: -99.5934)
  let northeast = CLLocationCoordinate2D(
      latitude: 30.8611,
      longitude: -96.6051)
  return MGLCoordinateBounds(sw: southwest,
                             ne: northeast)
}
```

The preceding method returns an `MGLCoordinateBounds` structure. You can also call `mapView.visibleCoordinateBounds` to get the bounds for the map displaying in the map view. You might know that your application serves a certain geographic area, in which case you might want to define fixed coordinates. Or you may let the user decide which tiles to download by picking an area out on the map themselves and then tapping a download button.

Once you have a set of bounds, you can create an `MGLTilePyramidOfflineRegion` region. These are the only types of offline regions you can create. They take the bounds, the minimum map zoom level, and the maximum map zoom level, as well as the map style to use. Typically, you would use the same map style as the map view, but you could specify another style URL if you like.

An example of creating a region looks like this:

```
let region = MGLTilePyramidOfflineRegion(
    styleURL: mapView.styleURL,
    bounds: bounds,
    fromZoomLevel: 5,
    toZoomLevel: 8)
```

We will use this code snippet in a method that downloads an offline map pack, so don't put it into your class yet.

The next step is to add an offline map pack. The MGLOfflineStorage class is a singleton (accessed with MGLOfflineStorage.shared) that you can call the addPack method on. This method takes the region, a context, and a completion handler. The context argument is a general-purpose storage variable that takes a Data instance. You can put anything you like into the context. We're going to take the simple approach and store a string as the context with UTF-8 encoding. The completion handler takes the offline pack and an error as optional arguments. Once you get the offline pack, call the resume() method on the pack to start the download process.

The complete method to download an offline map pack is in Listing 15-3. Add the downloadOfflineMapPack() method to your ViewController class. To test your code, call this method at the end of your viewDidLoad() method.

Listing 15-3. Download an offline map pack

```
func downloadOfflineMapPack() {
  let bounds = createOfflineRegionBounds()
  let region = MGLTilePyramidOfflineRegion(
    styleURL: mapView.styleURL,
    bounds: bounds,
    fromZoomLevel: 5,
    toZoomLevel: 8)
```

```
let packName = "Central Texas"
guard let nameData = packName.data(using: .utf8) else {
  return
}

MGLOfflineStorage.shared.addPack(
  for: region,
  withContext: nameData) { (pack, error) in
    guard let pack = pack else {
      print("Unable to create pack")
      print(error?.localizedDescription ??
        "No error given")
      return
    }
    pack.resume()
  }
}
```

You can specify your own offline map pack name; it is only used for reference by your own project. You could store a GUID there or a dictionary of name/value attributes.

Typically, you will want to know when the download process is finished, or you may want to display progress to the user. Let's take a look at the notifications that get sent when the Mapbox SDK downloads an offline map pack.

The complete code for the view controller is in Listing 15-4, if you want to see how each of the pieces fits together.

Monitoring offline map pack downloads

There are three different notifications that the offline map downloader will send out. These are standard iOS notifications, monitored with the NotificationCenter, not to be confused with push notifications:

- `MGLOfflinePackProgressChanged`

- `MGLOfflinePackError`

- `MGLOfflinePackMaximumMapboxTilesReached`

Let's focus on the progress changed notification. We need to subscribe to these progress changed notifications in our `viewDidLoad()` method. Add the code in the following snippet to your `viewDidLoad()` method:

```
NotificationCenter.default.addObserver(
  self,
  selector: #selector(offlinePackProgressChanged),
  name: NSNotification.Name.MGLOfflinePackProgressChanged,
  object: nil)
```

We also need to define that `offlinePackProgressChanged` method and make sure it has an `@objc` annotation. Add the following function definition to your class:

```
@objc func offlinePackProgressChanged(
  notification: NSNotification) {
  print("Offline pack progress changed")
}
```

If you go ahead and add the notification, observer in the `viewDidLoad()` method, and then add the `offlinePackProgressChanged()` method, run the app in the Simulator. You will see many print statements showing that something is happening!

If we want to get more details, we can get those from the
notification. The optional object property of the notification is the
offline pack. The offline pack has a property named progress that is an
MGLOfflinePackProgress structure. Let's print out those completed bytes
to the console:

```
@objc func offlinePackProgressChanged(
  notification: NSNotification) {
  guard let pack = notification.object
    as? MGLOfflinePack else {
      return
  }
  print("Offline pack progress changed")
  print(pack.progress.countOfBytesCompleted)
}
```

Modifying the function to show this will give us more information
about the progress of the application, but of course isn't quite ready for the
end users yet. They would probably like to see some kind of percentage,
letting them know that they are close to the finish. You can set this up with
a progress view, but for now we will simply print the percentages out, to the
console. Add the following to the end of the offlinePackProgressChanged
method:

```
let percentageResources = Int(round(100 *
    Float(progress.countOfResourcesCompleted) /
    Float(progress.countOfResourcesExpected)))

print("Resources: \(percentageResources)%")
```

To use this with a progress view, you could simply set the progress value of the progress view to be the number of resources completed divided by the number of resources expected:

```
progressView.progress = Float(progress.
countOfResourcesCompleted) /
    Float(progress.countOfResourcesExpected)))
```

Once the count of resources completed equals the number of count expected, you could dismiss the progress bar with a timer and optionally pop up an alert view.

Once we combine all of our code together, we end up with a view controller class, that will display a Mapbox map, but all of the download progress will be displayed on the console for debugging. The complete code listing for the ViewController class is in Listing 15-4.

Listing 15-4. Complete ViewController class

```
import UIKit
import Mapbox

class ViewController: UIViewController {

  @IBOutlet weak var mapView: MGLMapView!
  var progressView: UIProgressView!

  override func viewDidLoad() {
    super.viewDidLoad()
    // Do any additional setup after loading the view.
    mapView.centerCoordinate = CLLocationCoordinate2D(
            latitude: 30.2,
            longitude: -97.75)
    mapView.zoomLevel = 10
    mapView.styleURL = MGLStyle.outdoorsStyleURL
```

```swift
    NotificationCenter.default.addObserver(
        self,
        selector: #selector(offlinePackProgressChanged),
        name: NSNotification.Name.
        MGLOfflinePackProgressChanged,
        object: nil)

    downloadOfflineMapPack()
}

@objc func offlinePackProgressChanged(
    notification: NSNotification) {
    guard let pack = notification.object
        as? MGLOfflinePack else {
        return
    }

    let progress = pack.progress
    print("Offline pack progress changed")
    print(progress.countOfBytesCompleted)
    let percentageResources = Int(round(100 *
      Float(progress.countOfResourcesCompleted) /
      Float(progress.countOfResourcesExpected)))

    print("Resources: \(percentageResources)%")
}

func createOfflineRegionBounds() -> MGLCoordinateBounds {
  let southwest = CLLocationCoordinate2D(
      latitude: 28.822,
      longitude: -99.5934)
  let northeast = CLLocationCoordinate2D(
      latitude: 30.8611,
      longitude: -96.6051)
```

```
    return MGLCoordinateBounds(sw: southwest,
                                ne: northeast)
}

func downloadOfflineMapPack() {
  let bounds = createOfflineRegionBounds()
  let region = MGLTilePyramidOfflineRegion(
      styleURL: mapView.styleURL,
      bounds: bounds,
      fromZoomLevel: 5,
      toZoomLevel: 8)

  let packName = "Central Texas"
  guard let nameData = packName.data(using: .utf8) else {
    return
  }

  MGLOfflineStorage.shared.addPack(
    for: region,
    withContext: nameData) { (pack, error) in
        guard let pack = pack else {
          print("Unable to create pack")
          print(error?.localizedDescription ??
            "No error given")
          return
        }
      pack.resume()
  }
 }
}
```

Considerations for using offline map tiles

When you set up an application to use offline map tiles, there are several constraints to consider. The first is pricing. Make sure that you have an idea of how many tiles each user will download and how that fits into your budget. Use this number to drive the maximum zoom level or the maximum size of the map region. Also consider how long it will take for the user to perform the download. If you block the user from continuing into the application while the map tiles download, provide a progress bar or some other user interface. If the number of map tiles is large, let the user know that they should initiate the process themselves when they have access to a wireless Ethernet network, unless they want to incur large bandwidth charges from their carrier.

Mapbox does provide some soft limits to how many map tiles a user can download. That number is currently 6000 map tiles across all downloaded regions, but you can raise it yourself by calling the setMaximumAllowedMapboxTiles method on the MGLOfflineStorage class. Once you bump up against the built-in limit or the limit that you set, the Mapbox SDK will post the MGLOfflinePackMaximumMapboxTilesReached notification. You can listen for that notification similarly to how we listened for offline map tile download progress. Your app will have to remove existing offline map packs to continue downloading map tiles into a new pack if the limit is reached.

Last, Mapbox does not allow offline map tiles to be redistributed from the app (for instance, to another copy of the app on another user's phone), so read the terms of service to make sure that your app's overall design works with Mapbox's solution.

Index

A, B

addMarker method, 112, 161

API key
- AppDelegate.swift, 98
- bundle identifier, 96
- create credentials, 95
- creating project, 94
- creation dialog box, 96
- Google Maps Platform, 93
- iOS Maps, 98
- restriction, 97
- runtime error, 98

Apple's local search
- guard let, 44
- naturalLanguageQuery, 42
- pointOfInterestFilter, 42
- region, 42
- resultTypes, 42
- searching for points of interest, 43
- start method, 43
- web-accessible API, 41

application(_:didFinishLaunching WithOptions:) method, 147

Application programming interfaces (APIs), 1

C

autocompleteBounds property, 153

autocompleteFilter property, 155

calculate()/calculateETA() method, 54, 56

canShowCallout property, 38

Category filter, map annotations, 49, 50

CocoaPods, 222
- dependency manager, 90
- installation, 91
- NPM, 90
- Podfile, 91, 92
- Xcode workspace, 92, 93

Codable protocol, 127

coordinate property, 28

CoreLocation framework, 17, 20, 26

createWaypoints() method, 227

Creating annotation, search result, 47

Custom annotation class
- init method, 28
- map view, 30

D, E

F

G, H

Printed in the United States
By Bookmasters

Communications
in Computer and Information Science 558

Commenced Publication in 2007
Founding and Former Series Editors:
Alfredo Cuzzocrea, Dominik Ślęzak, and Xiaokang Yang

More information about this series at http://www.springer.com/series/7899

Lin Liu · Mikio Aoyama (Eds.)

Requirements Engineering in the Big Data Era

Second Asia Pacific Symposium, APRES 2015
Wuhan, China, October 18–20, 2015
Proceedings

 Springer

Editors
Lin Liu
Tsinghua University
Beijing
China

Mikio Aoyama
Department of Software Engineering
Nanzan University
Japan

ISSN 1865-0929 ISSN 1865-0937 (electronic)
Communications in Computer and Information Science
ISBN 978-3-662-48633-7 ISBN 978-3-662-48634-4 (eBook)
DOI 10.1007/978-3-662-48634-4

Library of Congress Control Number: 2015950926

Springer Heidelberg New York Dordrecht London

Printed on acid-free paper

Springer-Verlag GmbH Berlin Heidelberg is part of Springer Science+Business Media
(www.springer.com)

Lin Liu · Mikio Aoyama (Eds.)

Requirements Engineering in the Big Data Era

Second Asia Pacific Symposium, APRES 2015
Wuhan, China, October 18–20, 2015
Proceedings

 Springer

Editors
Lin Liu
Tsinghua University
Beijing
China

Mikio Aoyama
Department of Software Engineering
Nanzan University
Japan

ISSN 1865-0929   ISSN 1865-0937 (electronic)
Communications in Computer and Information Science
ISBN 978-3-662-48633-7   ISBN 978-3-662-48634-4 (eBook)
DOI 10.1007/978-3-662-48634-4

Library of Congress Control Number: 2015950926

Springer Heidelberg New York Dordrecht London

Printed on acid-free paper

Springer-Verlag GmbH Berlin Heidelberg is part of Springer Science+Business Media
(www.springer.com)